HAMLET

By the same author:

Conrad's 'Heart of Darkness': A Critical and Contextual Discussion, 1977
Cunninghame Graham: A Critical Biography (with Laurence Davies), 1979
A Preface to Conrad, 1982
R. B. Cunninghame Graham, 1983
The Deceptive Text: An Introduction to Covert Plots, 1984
A Preface to Keats, 1985
William Shakespeare: 'Measure for Measure', 1986

Edited by the same author:

Joseph Conrad's Letters to R. B. Cunninghame Graham, 1969
The English Novel, 1976
Selected Writings of Cunninghame Graham, 1981
Joseph Conrad: 'Lord Jim' (with Robert Hampson), 1986
Joseph Conrad: 'Typhoon' and Other Tales, 1986
Joseph Conrad: 'The Nigger of the "Narcissus"', 1988

Harvester New Critical Introductions
to Shakespeare

HAMLET

Cedric Watts

Professor of English, University of Sussex

HARVESTER · WHEATSHEAF
NEW YORK LONDON TORONTO SYDNEY TOKYO

12983

First published 1988 by
Harvester · Wheatsheaf
66 Wood Lane End, Hemel Hempstead,
Hertfordshire HP2 4RG

A division of Simon & Schuster International Group

Printed and bound in Great Britain by Billing and
Sons Limited, Worcester

British Library Cataloguing in Publication Data

Watts, Cedric
    Hamlet.—(Harvester new critical
    introductions to Shakespeare).
    1. Shakespeare, William. Hamlet
    I. Title   II. Shakespeare, William.
    Hamlet
    822.3′3

    ISBN 0-7108-1143-8
    ISBN 0-7108-1157-8 Pbk

1 2 3 4 5   92 91 90 89 88

Titles in the Series

GENERAL EDITOR: GRAHAM BRADSHAW

General Editor's Preface

The *New Critical Introductions to Shakespeare* series will include studies of all Shakespeare's plays, together with two volumes on the non-dramatic verse, and is designed to offer a challenge to all students of Shakespeare.

Each volume will be brief enough to read in an evening, but long enough to avoid those constraints which are inevitable in articles and short essays. Each contributor will develop a sustained critical reading of the play in question, which addresses those difficulties and critical disagreements which each play has generated.

Different plays present different problems, different challenges and excitements. In isolating these, each volume will present a preliminary survey of the play's stage history and critical reception. The volumes then provide a more extended discussion of these matters in the main text, and of matters relating to genre, textual problems and the use of source material, or to historical and theoretical issues. But here, rather than setting a row of dragons at the gate, we have assumed that 'background' should figure only as it emerges into a critical foreground; part of the critical endeavour is to establish, and sift, those issues which seem most pressing.

So, for example, when Shakespeare determined that *his* Othello and Desdemona should have no time to live together, or that Cordelia dies while Hermione survives, his deliberate departures from his source material have a critical significance which is often blurred, when discussed in the context of lengthily detailed surveys of 'the sources'. Alternatively, plays like *The Merchant of Venice* or *Measure for Measure* show Shakespeare welding together different 'stories' from quite different sources, so that their relation to each other becomes a matter for critical debate. And Shakespeare's dramatic practice poses different critical questions when we ask—or if we ask: few do—why particular characters in a poetic drama speak only in verse or only in prose; or when we try to engage with those recent, dauntingly specialised and controversial textual studies which set out to establish the evidence for authorial revisions or joint authorship. We all read *King Lear* and *Macbeth*, but we are not all textual critics; nor are textual critics always able to show where their arguments have critical consequences which concern us all.

Just as we are not all textual critics, we are not all linguists, cultural anthropologists, psychoanalysts or New Historicists. The diversity of contemporary approaches to Shakespeare is unprecedented, enriching, bewildering. One aim of this series is to represent what is illuminating in this diversity. As the hastiest glance through the list of contributors will confirm, the series does not attempt to 're-read' Shakespeare by placing an ideological grid over the text and reporting on whatever shows through. Nor would the series' contributors always agree with each other's arguments, or premises; but each has been invited to develop a sustained critical argument which will also provide its own critical and historical context—by taking account of those issues which have perplexed or divided audiences, readers, and critics past and present.

Graham Bradshaw

Contents

Preface

THE PLAN OF THIS BOOK

Hamlet is notoriously problematic, so my intention is not to offer yet another 'solution' of the play's mystery but, instead, to attempt an explanation of its mysteriousness. A pretentious title for the project might be 'The Dynamics of the Problematic of *Hamlet*'; a clearer title would be 'An Explanation of *Hamlet*'s Evident Tendency to Solicit and Frustrate Explanations'. By thus seeking an overview of the contenders, rather than hastening to advocate a fresh contention, we may learn a little more about Shakespeare's play and possibly about other perplexing texts.

In the case of *Hamlet*, the 'dynamics of the problematic' evidently require the following items:

1. The presence of commentators who are committed to maximising the intelligibility of the play, particularly of the play regarded as text rather than as performance.
2. Evidence, within much of the text, of a high level of intelligent co-ordination.
3. Evidence, within parts of the text, of an absence of intelligent co-ordination; indeed, signs of apparent confusion or contradiction.
4. Textual material which has an uncertain status, so that commentators will wrangle about its possible reallocation to categories 2 or 3.

Similarly, the characterisation of Hamlet himself exhibits much co-ordination, some confusion or contradiction, and some indeterminate material. The last includes an area of opacity which is made conspicuous (or generated) by the character's declared perplexity concerning its content.

The preliminary sections of this book give examples of items 1 and 4 listed above. Chapter 1 illustrates item 3. Chapter 2 illustrates item 2, and Chapter 3 offers a conclusion. The summing-up emphasises that *Hamlet* tends to be far less problematic in the theatre than it is in the study, and that the pleasures of the play are less dependent on demonstrably logical co-ordination than commentators have usually assumed. Both by accident and by design, *Hamlet* properly remains protean.

'IS THIS A PRÓLOGUE . . . . .?'

Hamlet: cue for critical clichés: one of Shakespeare's greatest tragedies and one of the world's literary masterpieces; vivid, profound, mysterious; its protagonist the most enigmatic character in the history of drama. The *Hamlet* industry continues to expand; experts claim that this play has generated a greater quantity of discussion, exegesis, scholarly controversy and textual debate than any other; Hamlet himself has exerted a powerfully varied cultural influence; and the play defiantly retains its vitality on stage, while reaching mass audiences via the cinema and television.

By now it is a text burdened with the massive weight of its own fame, blurred by the vast aureole of its own glory, and haunted by the long reputation of its enigma; doomed to quote and mimic itself. Sometimes the most humble (yet, given the difficulty, most arrogant) task for a critic may seem to be that of rescuing *Hamlet* from its own prestige; redeeming it from its own glamour.

As it has survived to us, *Hamlet* is partly a botched and unfinished work, scruffily untidy and clumsily inconsistent.

It is also, partly but impressively, a highly co-ordinated, subtly organised entity. And that combination of the two things—the lack of co-ordination and the brilliance of co-ordination—has largely generated so much of the discussion and speculation. The play keeps more promises than we expect it to make; it makes more promises that it keeps. If much of it seems intelligent and part seems stupid, naturally we worry away at the seemingly stupid in the hope of discovering that it is, after all, intelligent. If much is co-ordinated and part seems a muddle, we worry at the muddle in the hope that it will reveal itself to be co-ordinated. The rich diversity of *Hamlet* can project images of an ideal, clarified *Hamlet*; and audiences, directors, commentators and critics are again and again tempted to realise that ideal: the play's pregnancy breeds midwives. Hamlet seeks, in frustration and anguish, a reason for his delay, and we try to help him: how about this reason? or that? or another? He's magnanimous, yet he's spiteful; he's sensitive, yet brutal; noble, yet hysterical; and we try to resolve him: he's really this, we'll say, or essentially that, or unconsciously something else.

One reason why Hamlet is such a popular role for aspiring actors is that he brazenly solicits interpretation. He provides so much, he offers such diversity, he's a virtuoso welcoming virtuosi, a performer harshly reviewing his performance; yet he has his lacunae, his reticences; he offers spaces to be filled. The play challenges directors as few others do, being prestigious yet uneven, spectacular yet erratic; a play about plays: isn't its hero himself a director, throwing a gauntlet to fellow-directors? *Hamlet* seduces audiences, being a lithe lubricated classic that mocks the stiff pomposity of other classics; varied and lively in pace, with a rapid sequence of contrasting scenes; its minor roles distinct as cameos, the hero diversifying himself into many roles; the whole combining simple and time-tested theatrical pleasures with subtly taxing interpretative riddles. And isn't it a play about theatre-goers, about critics, about assessment of performances? As a tragedy, it's a mishmash of old and new, melodrama and realism, passion and meditation; the ingredients include love, death, sex, even incest, the supernatural, politics, intrigue, youth and age, innocence and experience, piety and scepticism, absurdity and pathos, and—one of the strangest—historical prolepsis: for this Renaissance play has the effrontery to address, and even generate, the modern and contemporary.

'Who's there?' 'Nay, answer me. Stand and unfold yourself.' The play's characteristic grammatical mood, established in its first line, is the interrogative: it questions life, art, the audience, and the reader's tidy categorisations. Some of Shakespeare's tragedies have a consistent generic poise: however rich and intense may be *Romeo and Juliet*, *Julius Caesar*, *Macbeth* or *Antony and Cleopatra*, they do not threaten to subvert their own fictional premises. Some of the other works categorised as tragedies—*Hamlet*, *Troilus and Cressida* and *King Lear*—do wield that subversive quality: they fret at conventional literary-generic bounds and divisions. Hamlet is generically dangerous: he's capable of sabotaging the action's tragic dignity. By some obvious criteria, *Hamlet* belongs to the genre of revenge drama; but again the play seems waywardly determined to resist its own generic origins; indeed, the plight of Hamlet himself, burdened by an unavoidable yet uncongenial task, may seem to be inflected by the plight of the author, Shakespeare, veering and erring within the constraints of a necessary yet in some ways uncongenial task of literary adaptation.

One reason for *Hamlet*'s power to elicit so much scholarly and interpretative energy is simply that the earliest extant texts constitute a multiple muddle. No single early text is satisfactory as it stands; editors struggle to make a coherent synthesis from chunks of one text and bits of others. Even the best of the early versions, the Second Quarto, provides a play which, though lengthy and meaty, contains inconsistencies and contradictions, as if the script had been trapped prematurely in type before due revision and final ordering. So the scholars labour on Shakespeare's behalf (as they presume), seeking to realise a more stable and harmonious text. Often they may, for all their labours, be taking us further away from the true *Hamlet*, which may never have been a fixed and finished but rather a variable and pliable body of material, repeatedly being revised, adapted, cut, augmented and permutated in the light of immediate theatrical exigencies and the changing interests of contrasting audiences. Christopher Marlowe's *Tragicall History of the Life and Death of Doctor Faustus* seems (to judge from the big differences between the 'A Text' and the 'B Text') to have metamorphosed into something resembling *The Doctor Faustus Road-Show*; and Shakespeare's *Hamlet* was doubtless staged not only in lavish and ample productions but also in cheap, abridged and garbled versions—as by those touring companies in Europe who helped to generate the eighteenth-century German version known as *Der Bestrafte Brudermord*.

Another reason for the scale of the interpretative endeavour is that the text of *Hamlet* contains so much material which, if not digressive, may at first appear so, since this material seems to proliferate to the side (or over the edge) of the predictable course of the action; prince and play flow to excess; so commentators who value or overvalue unity may struggle with that superflux to try to render it less wayward and more conventionally functional. Yet in doing so they may be defeating the play's distinctively radical realism. The prince's own literary views suggest that *Hamlet* is, among many other things, an experiment in realism; and in that respect it's a culturally proleptic drama, markedly more so than some of Shakespeare's later works. Frequently, in literature, what induces a sense of realism is the accommodation of the unexpectedly wayward detail: the functional (because lifelike or searching) deployment of the seemingly unfunctional—of matter which seems to lack predictable literary function. Consequently one of the most delicate tasks for a critic may be that of discriminating between what, in the early texts, is really erroneous or botched, and what results from a deliberate endeavour to challenge conventional notions of exposition. A melody which in a standard commercial orchestration is banal can provide an accomplished jazz-musician with the basis for intense, innovatory, searching improvisations. Perhaps in *Hamlet*, more than in any other of his plays, Shakespeare comes closest to proclaiming that it isn't the received plot that matters, it's what is done with it: an ancient legend has provided a basis for new improvisations of imagination which, caught in changing states on paper, then provide the materials for stage performances which themselves always partake of the improvised. Hamlet may not be a tragic hero trapped in a mere revenge drama, but he can give the uncanny impression of being a real person who, in a credibly skewed world, is more interested in the improvisations his situation licenses than in conventional obedience to the role and the plot that have been issued to him. He's a modern jazzman at heart (pity he couldn't practise on the alto-sax instead of the rapier): so he may seem to someone preoccupied with jazz. To a psycho-analyst, he'll be a man with an Oedipus Complex who badly needs a course of therapy; to a Christian, he may be a seeker who at last becomes reconciled to divine providence; to sceptics, he may be a pioneering sceptic; to intellectual procrastinators, a procrastinating intellectual. It's notorious that he seems to change to fit the predilections of the observer—either to mirror the observer's ideals or to match the observer's covert failings. One reason why so many critics take such a personal interest in Hamlet is not just that he's extraordinarily diverse, complex and contradictory, offering so wide a range of views that his character is bound to seem symbiotic with ours; it's that his attitudes, actions and ideas never seem to receive, in the play, the comprehension and clarification that they solicit, and hence our responses may become fraternally possessive: we seek to supply the interpretation he repeatedly invites and which nobody in the fictional world seems fully competent to give. He ambushes, frames and tantalises us.

> You would play upon me, you would seem to know my stops, you would pluck out the heart of my mystery . . . . . Call me what instrument you will, though you fret me, you cannot play upon me.

Thus for centuries the critics have been emulating Rosencrantz and Guildenstern by seeking to play on Hamlet and pluck out the heart of the mystery. In all this critical activity there's much that's admirable and even poignant. Living people seek to lend part of their life-energies to a fictional character; industrious scholars and directors seek to collaborate with the imagination of a playwright who died in 1616. There's also something ludicrous: chapfallen Yorick mutely mocks the generations of loquacious sages who haggle over rival interpretations or solemnly analyse the blunders and guesswork of haphazard Elizabethan compositors. There may even be something immoral: in a world where each year countless children die for want of food and medicine, our garbled values and perverse economic systems permit money and energy to be devoted to the service of a dead dramatist and his fictional offspring. Nevertheless, there are many worse devotions. Shakespeare extended—generally for the better—the definition of the human: he offered enduring images of articulate intelligence, imagination and sensitivity; he helped to create the very conscience which can be troubled by the spectacle of the Shakespeare industry. 'Use every man after his desert, and who shall scape whipping?'

Acknowledgements

Quotations from *Hamlet* are from the Arden edition edited by Harold Jenkins (London and New York: Methuen, 1982). Quotations from other Shakespearian texts are from *The Complete Works* edited by Peter Alexander (the 'Tudor' edition; London and Glasgow: Collins, 1951; reprinted 1966).

In any quotation, a row of three dots indicates an ellipsis already present in the printed text, whereas a row of five dots indicates an omission that I have made. In lines of verse, I have where necessary inserted a grave accent over any otherwise-unsounded syllable that needs to be sounded in order to preserve the metre. All other emendations to quoted passages are enclosed in square brackets. With these exceptions, I have endeavoured to present all quoted material without correction or alteration.

This book was written in 1986; Alan Sinfield kindly provided constructive criticism and helped to check the proofs.

The Stage History

Over the centuries, in several continents and not merely in England, *Hamlet* has been performed innumerable times in countless ways, and has generated operas, ballets, travesties, films (including seventeen silent versions), radio and television productions, and 'transtextual' offspring like Stoppard's *Rosencrantz and Guildenstern Are Dead*. I first encountered *Hamlet* not as a text or a stage-play but as a mysterious and exciting film—the famous Olivier production, 1948; and even before my mother took me to see it, we knew the 'To be or not to be' soliloquy well from radio, because the Olivier recording had become a popular item on record-request programmes. Clearly, a comprehensive and up-to-date 'Stage History' would fill several volumes and would range far beyond the theatre; and there'd still be gaps, for many productions will have left no trace. So I'll briefly offer some samples which relate to the main critical thesis of the present book. First, samples from the earliest period.

Although Gabriel Harvey's *Marginalia* (c. 1601) claimed that *Hamlet* could please 'the wiser sort', Antony Skoloker declared in 1604 that *Hamlet* was able to 'please all';[1] and his declaration gains support from the evident popularity of the play on stage during the seventeenth century. It was registered in 1602 as 'A booke . . . . . latelie Acted by the

Lord Chamberleyne his servantes'; the First Quarto stated
that it had been acted at the Universities of Oxford and
Cambridge, as well as at London; in 1619–20 it was
performed at Court; and in 1637 it was acted before King
Charles and Queen Henrietta.[2] Versions of *Hamlet* were
even performed at sea, as on Captain Keeling's ship *Dragon*:
in 1608 Keeling noted, 'I envited Captain Hawkins to a ffishe
dinner, and had Hamlet acted abord me: w[hi]ch I p[er]mitt
to keepe my people from idlenes and unlawfull games, or
sleepe'[3]—a frank admission of the utility of drama as an
instrument of social control. During the 1660s Samuel
Pepys attended productions of the play on several
occasions, was particularly delighted by Betterton's
performances in the title-role, and learnt by heart the 'To be
or not to be' passage.[4] Betterton's acting was also praised by
Nicolas Rowe, who, in the introduction to his edition of the
works (1709), referred to *Hamlet* as 'this Master-piece of
Shakespear' and claimed that Shakespeare himself had
formerly taken the part of the ghost. By 1711 Lord
Shaftesbury could describe the play as 'that piece of his
which appears to have most affected English hearts, and has
perhaps been oftenest acted of any which have come upon
our stage'.[5] Altogether, then, solid evidence of *Hamlet*'s
great popularity with a diversity of audiences, and a
reminder of its own diversity in practice.

During the eighteenth century, celebrated performers of
Hamlet included Wilks, Barry, Garrick, Henderson and
Kemble; and all of them, in varying degrees, maintained the
tradition of textual surgery that had been well established in
Betterton's   day   and   which,   indeed,   was   quite
Shakespearian—Hamlet himself was willing to send a script
'to the barber's'. Hamlet's speeches were commonly
abbreviated; his advice to the players was sometimes
omitted, while some characters (Cornelius, Voltemand,
Reynaldo, Fortinbras) might vanish entirely. By 1772
Garrick's version dispensed with the grave-diggers, the
funeral of Ophelia, the voyage to England, and Laertes' plot.

Another late-eighteenth-century development (maintained until the early twentieth century) was the casting of a woman in the leading role. The part of Hamlet was played by Sarah Siddons, Mrs Inchbald and Jane Powell; their example was followed by Julia Glover, Charlotte Cushman, Alice Marriott, Bella Pateman, Clara Howard, Millicent Bandmann-Palmer, Sarah Bernhardt, Eva Le Gallienne and Asta Nielsen; as late as 1938, the part was taken by Esmé Beringer.[6] Given that Ophelia and Gertrude were originally played by boys, this seems an appropriate cultural riposte, though not necessarily with feminist implications: Hamlet's sensitivity and vacillation were often deemed feminesque, and E. P. Vining's *The Mystery of Hamlet* (1861) offered the theory that Hamlet was really a woman who had suffered the misfortune of being brought up as a man.

Meanwhile, on stage in the twentieth century, *Hamlet* grew in prestige, being a celebrated 'star vehicle' for Henry Irving, Martin Harvey, Johnston Forbes-Robertson, Godfrey Tearle, John Gielgud, Alec Guinness, Alec Clunes, Donald Wolfit, Laurence Olivier, Michael Redgrave, Richard Burton, Nicol Williamson, Ian McKellen, David Warner, Derek Jacobi, Jonathan Pryce; repeatedly the main role was seen as one of that select group by which a skilled player could rapidly establish or confirm his stature as a major actor. '[T]he part has become a hoop through which aspiring classical actors have to jump', observed Jacobi.[7] The role demands stamina, range, subtlety, vigour; it greedily dominates the play; and since every performance is a re-interpretation, a criticism and partly an improvisation, there's always something new to be done. Film versions have shown Hamlet played by a woman (Sarah Bernhardt, Asta Nielsen), a man (notably Forbes-Robertson, Olivier and Smoktunovsky) and even two men simultaneously (twins: Anthony and David Meyer). One director with experience of filming Shakespeare's works, Peter Hall, has remarked:

When you consider a major achievement of writing such as a play by Shakespeare, you are continually reinterpreting it. This object is there and it's like a sputnik, it turns round, and over the years different portions of it are nearer to you, different bits are further away. It's rushing past and you are peeling off those meanings. In that way a text is dynamic. The whole question of what Shakespeare intended doesn't arise, because what he has written not only carries more meanings than he consciously intended, but those meanings are altered in a mysterious way as the text moves through the centuries. If you dig into it you find some new aspect, and yet you never seize the thing itself.[8]

In the next section, we shall see various attempts to 'seize the thing itself'; and this book will proceed to discuss the text's peculiar power to solicit a search for what does not exist: the essential *Hamlet*.

The Critical History

The previous section has already emphasised that the distinction between 'Stage History' and 'Critical History' is arbitrary, since every production of *Hamlet* entails processes of evaluation and interpretation. As previously, I'll select samples which relate to the main argument of this book.

Before 1736 detailed analyses of the play were rare, though there was a consensus that it succeeded admirably. But in 1736, in an anonymous essay sometimes attributed to Thomas Hanmer, *Hamlet* was deemed problematic in its structure and its details, and the prince's delay was seen as crucially ill-motivated:

> To speak Truth, our Poet, by keeping too close to the Ground-work of his Plot, has fallen into an Absurdity; for there appears no Reason at all in Nature, why the young Prince did not put the Usurper to Death as soon as possible, especially as *Hamlet* is represented as a Youth so brave, and so careless of his own Life.
>
> The Case indeed is this: Had *Hamlet* gone naturally to work, as we could suppose such a Prince to do in parallel Circumstances, there would have been an End of our Play. The Poet therefore was obliged to delay his Hero's

Revenge; but then he should have contrived some good
Reason for it.[1]

In France, where neoclassical tastes sustained Racine's
reputation, Voltaire condemned *Hamlet* as largely vulgar
and barbarous.[2] Dr Johnson answered Voltaire generally by
emphasising Shakespeare's realism, his concern for 'nature'
rather than convention: 'This therefore is the praise of
Shakespeare, that his drama is the mirror of life'—an echo
of Hamlet's own precept. Johnson did, however, say that
though *Hamlet* is lively, varied and instructive, it incurs
objections: the prince's feigned madness appears to have 'no
adequate cause', his treatment of Ophelia entails 'useless
and wanton cruelty', he is 'an instrument rather than an
agent', the catastrophe is fortuitous, and 'The apparition left
the regions of the dead to little purpose; the revenge which
he demands is not obtained but by the death of him that was
required to take it'.[3] Thus the play was now confirmed as
problematic, and its protagonist began to manifest his talent
for prolepsis—for anticipating emergent cultural phases and
fashions. In the latter half of the eighteenth century, as the
'Cult of Sensibility' burgeoned, Hamlet seemed a
progenitor of the fashionable cult of pensive sensitivity, and
attention focused on the mystery of his delay in obeying the
call of vengeance. The fashion proffered the solution:
William Richardson in 1774 argued influentially that
Hamlet's nature was too refined and sensitive for the harsh
task imposed upon it;[4] Henry Mackenzie (author of the
popular sentimental novel, *The Man of Feeling*) claimed that
Hamlet exhibited 'an extreme sensibility of mind, apt to be
strongly impressed by its situation, and overpowered by the
feelings which that situation excites';[5] and Goethe
concurred in seeing an over-sensitive soul burdened with an
inappropriate task: 'A lovely, pure, noble and highly moral
nature, lacking heroic toughness, sinks beneath a burden
which it can neither bear not throw off'.[6]
In the early nineteenth century, the spate of character-

studies of Hamlet testified to the prince's anticipation of the romantic movement's enthusiasm for intense individualism. Both Coleridge and Hazlitt saw the prince as essentially a thinker, not a doer; an intellectual incapacitated by his reflective temperament. Coleridge declared, 'He is a man living in meditation, called upon to act by every motive human and divine, but the great object of his life is defeated by continually resolving to do, yet doing nothing but resolve.'[7] Understandably, this prince of introspective inertia sired many offspring in Tsarist Russia, among them Turgenev's 'The Hamlet of the Schigorov District' and Chekhov's 'A Moscow Hamlet'; while, in the lecture 'Hamlet and Don Quixote' (1860), Turgenev declared that in these two figures we see 'the twin antitypes of human nature, the two poles of the axle-tree on which that nature turns'.[8] Hamlet, he claimed, is too sceptical to believe in the goals of action, and thus is unable to act, while Don Quixote is able to act impetuously, but only because he irrationally sees windmills as giants. This lecture is a good illustration of the way in which so many nineteenth-century writers and artists sought to compensate Hamlet for his loss of the throne of Denmark by conferring on him the status of literary archetype, alongside Oedipus, Faust, Don Juan, Don Quixote and Robinson Crusoe—all of them being figures who embody, in perilous excess, a widespread ambition or power. Eventually, Hamlet was even addressed (by Anatole France) as the modern Everyman:

You belong to every era and every country . . . . . It has even been claimed, my prince, that you are an emporium of thoughts, a mass of contradictions, and not a human being. But, on the contrary, that is the sign of your profound humanity. You are quick and slow, bold and fearful, kind and cruel, you believe and you doubt, you are wise and above all you are mad. Which of us does not resemble you in some respect? Which of us thinks without contradiction and acts without incoherence? Which of us is not mad?[9]

France's declaration usefully exposes the rules of the critical game which was to continue without foreseeable termination. Some critics (often the more scholarly analysts or editors) see contradictions in the play, and particularly in Hamlet himself; other critics are then provoked to discover some principle of co-ordination, usually by postulating a coherent 'biography' of the prince, sometimes by claiming (as France did, and as post-structuralists were to do) that the contradictions are actually 'true to life'. In the next section we'll consider some twentieth-century players of this vast, earnest, ludicrous and poignant game.

SOME TWENTIETH-CENTURY VIEWS

Hamlet: Melancholic, Hybrid, Immature, Cruel?

The most influential twentieth-century discussion of *Hamlet* was probably A. C. Bradley's in *Shakespearean Tragedy* (1904), a strenuous attempt to make the text conform to the ancient and traditional notion that a great work of literature should be 'an organic whole', rationally coherent and explicable. In keeping with his times, the era of William James's *Principles of Psychology* and of rapid progress in psychiatry and psycho-analysis, Bradley finds that the secret of the tragedy lies in Hamlet's psychology, and particularly in the melancholy induced in his noble and idealistic nature by the moral shock of his mother's hasty remarriage. This melancholy accounts for Hamlet's inaction, since 'his habitual feeling is one of disgust at life and everything in it, himself included', yet (paradoxically)

this state accounts for Hamlet's energy as well as for his

lassitude, those quick decided actions of his being the outcome of a nature normally far from passive, now suddenly stimulated, and producing healthy impulses which work themselves out before they have time to subside.

It also accounts for 'his callousness, his insensibility to the fates of those whom he despises, and to the feelings even of those whom he loves. These are frequent symptoms of such melancholy'. Of course, 'this pathological condition' would be of little tragic interest if it were not accompanied by 'speculative genius'. It is the resultant combination of the power of thought and the powerlessness to act that gives the play its distinctive profundity: '*Hamlet* most brings home to us at once the sense of the soul's infinity, and the sense of the doom which not only circumscribes that infinity but appears to be its offspring.'[10]

Bradley's discussion is lengthy, sympathetic and eloquently persuasive, ranges confidently between general effects and particular details of the text, and must have given many readers the sense that they had at last gained a thoroughly comprehensive account of the main character and indeed of the meaning of the play. However, in A. J. A. Waldock's '*Hamlet*': *A Study in Critical Method* (1931) that account was systematically challenged.

Even if we were to accept Bradley's premises, says Waldock, we would not necessarily conclude that Hamlet's melancholy must lead to inaction; it would be as logical for a melancholy Hamlet to despatch Claudius rapidly; in addition to which, Hamlet does display bursts of activity (as Bradley had conceded), so that the causal argument is inconsistent. More importantly, Bradley's method is radically at fault: 'Drama is *not* history': instead of inferring a sequence of antecedent events, we should concentrate on what the words of the text actually say. At III.iii. 73–96, Hamlet refrains from killing the praying Claudius, explaining that he wishes to be sure of sending Claudius' soul to hell. Bradley had claimed that Hamlet was seeking a pretext for postponement, being inwardly reluctant to act. Yet, in Waldock's view, Hamlet means what he says: he really hopes to damn Claudius. Of course, modern audiences are likely to recoil from the direct, obvious meaning of the words, and Bradley's interpretation renders those words congenial to modern sensitivities; but congeniality does not entail validity. Again, when discussing the soliloquy which begins 'O, what a rogue and peasant slave am I' (II.ii. 544–601), Bradley claims that Hamlet's sudden doubt about the ghost's provenance is really another rationalisation of delay; but Waldock argues that such doubts about ghosts were currently discussed in Elizabethan England, and, in any case, the explanation of Hamlet's sudden wish to test the ghost is structural, not psychological:

> The next major event due in the plot is the play-scene. The concluding parts of this soliloquy provide the bridge to that scene. It is not, perhaps, a thoroughly sound bridge; if we step heavily on it, it gives alarmingly. If we slip by more lightly, it serves well enough.

In fact, the whole trouble with Bradley's version of the play is that it *improves* the original: 'Bradley's *Hamlet* is better than Shakespeare's: it is better in the sense that it has a firmer consistency, that it hangs together with a more irresistible logic.'[11] Waldock then develops the case previously advanced by C. M. Lewis, J. M. Robertson, Levin Schücking and E. E. Stoll: that Shakespeare's *Hamlet* is a hybrid, born of incompatible parents—the source-material and Shakespeare's additions to it. The inherited plot predominantly concerned revenge against the usurper; Shakespeare gives centrality to the son's disillusionment with his mother:

> [T]he revenge theme in the final play has been

considerably damaged . . . . . There are misfits. The old
material seems here and there to bulge out awkwardly
into the new play. Old consequences are retained, and
sometimes do not have their proper causes. Episodes lose
their *raison d'être* and inhere in the play like survivals.[12]

These 'survivals' include the swearing to secrecy and the
feigned madness: traditional or 'institutional' features of the
story which would seem natural enough when invoked,
even though the new setting made them pointless. Another
survival is the voyage to England, for which Shakespeare
provides no adequate reason; it clearly does not further
Hamlet's task; perhaps this traditional feature was included
because 'the actor playing the hero was badly in need of a
rest hereabouts'. As for the famous delay: it may have no
psychological reason at all; if there had been one,
Shakespeare would surely have told us; and, in the theatre,
the delay does not greatly matter. We should honestly
admit that the play is imperfect.

An old plot is wrenched to new significances,
significances, in places, that to the end it refuses to take
. . . . . Chords are sounded, dimly, suggestively, then
become blurred. We seem to gain partial visions of
intentions not clearly formulated . . . . . But what would
Hamlet be without its puzzles: the eternal piquancy of its
imperfection?[13]

Bradley had seen Hamlet as a consistent study in
melancholia; the reader might reflect that if that were the
case, there would surely have emerged, long before
Bradley's study, a critical consensus that melancholia was
clearly the explanation of Hamlet's conduct. And Waldock
was surely correct to point out that Bradley's account
placates modern humane sensibilities: it enables the reader
to say, 'If Hamlet does cruel things, that's because he isn't in
his right frame of mind; essentially he's a noble idealist

sorely afflicted'. On the other hand, if Bradley offered a *Hamlet* that was 'better than' Shakespeare's, defenders of Bradley might argue that Waldock's *Hamlet* is 'worse than' Shakespeare's, for here the enigma is reduced to a case of clumsy craftsmanship. (If 'archaic' material has survived, perhaps Shakespeare chose, for good reason, to let it do so.) Again, if Bradley went too far in constructing a Hamlet antecedent to the facts of the play, it could be argued that Waldock, by his concentration on the surface meaning of crucial speeches, has not gone far enough. If we accept the principle that a dramatic character can lie, deceive or be ironic, we thereby concede the principle that speeches in a play are not always to be taken literally but may properly be read in the light of our inference of an anterior or hidden self, the inferred self being one that maximises the general consistency and intelligibility of the character's words and actions as presented throughout the play. This principle is widely accepted, even by those critics who have denigrated Bradley's approach: notably by L. C. Knights.

In a famous essay of 1933, 'How Many Children Had Lady Macbeth?', Knights argued that it was improper to concentrate on characterisation in a Shakespeare play:

> In the mass of Shakespeare criticism there is not a hint that 'character'—like 'plot', 'rhythm', 'construction' and all our other critical counters—is merely an abstraction from the total response in the mind of the reader or spectator . . . . .[14]

And, accordingly, he offered a reading of *Macbeth* which emphasised that the play is really 'a poem': characterisation is subordinate to the total symbolic order of the work, and though we may intermittently think of the protagonist as 'a person in a play', we should give priority to the 'impersonal overtone'. In the essay 'Prince Hamlet' (1940), however, Knights's approach was remarkably Bradleian; and he excused this (in a way which demolished his previous case) by saying that whereas in *Macbeth* characterisation is subordinate to the total pattern, in other plays 'the hero's character . . . . . emerges from the pattern, and interest is centred there'. Then followed a reading of *Hamlet* which, though more hostile to the prince than Bradley's, still sought, as Bradley had done, to explain his mystery primarily in terms of his psychology:

> The desire to escape from the complexities of adult living is central to Hamlet's character . . . . . His attitudes of hatred, revulsion, self-complacence, and self-reproach . . . . . are, in their one-sided insistence, forms of escape from the difficult process of complex adjustment which normal living demands and which Hamlet finds beyond his powers.

Furthermore, Hamlet's immature attitudes seem not fully 'placed' or criticised within the text: possibly he expresses 'feelings that were personal to Shakespeare and not merely dramatically conceived':

> If this is so, it may help to explain why the 'negative' verse expressing loathing and recoil is, on the whole, so much more forceful than the passages in which any positive values are indicated. Ophelia's description of the earlier Hamlet [III.i. 152–62], like Hamlet's description of his hero-father [III.iv. 53–63], is weak and general compared with the astounding force and particularity of Hamlet's scathing comments on his mother's lust or on his uncle's guilt.

Of course, says Knights, most of us have 'a smack of Hamlet' in ourselves; but this is certainly not to our credit.

> *Hamlet* can provide an indulgence for some of our most cherished weaknesses—so deeply cherished that we can persuade ourselves that they are virtues—but it is

incapable of leading us far towards maturity and self-knowledge.[15]

We seem to have travelled, with Knights, a long way from Bradley's noble though melancholy prince. Knights's emphasis on the need for moral vigilance, for 'maturity and self-knowledge', reflects the influence of F. R. Leavis, to whose periodical, *Scrutiny*, Knights was a frequent contributor; and the essay on *Hamlet* also acknowledges a debt to G. Wilson Knight, who, in 'The Embassy of Death' (1930), had come close to depicting Hamlet as the villain of the piece. According to Wilson Knight, the 'surly Ghost' is 'the devil of the knowledge of death'; and the prince, corrupted by that knowledge, 'murders all the wrong people, exults in cruelty, grows more and more dangerous'. 'By creating normal and healthy and lovable persons around his protagonist, whose chief peculiarity is the abnormality of extreme melancholia, the poet divides our sympathies.'[16]

When we look back over this series of divergent views, it may appear that all of them, including L. C. Knights's, are subject to the daunting rule that Knights himself parenthetically formulated:

> *Hamlet* . . . . . contains within itself widely different levels of experience and insight which, since they cannot be assimilated into a whole, create a total effect of ambiguity. (This would help to explain why on different minds *Hamlet* can make such different impressions; since it offers unusually varied possibilities of interpretation you pick what pleases you and what your temperament demands.)[17]

T. S. Eliot and the Erratic Objective Correlative

T. S. Eliot's essay 'Hamlet' (1919) was a memorably

quotable polemical piece which roundly declared that
play is most certainly an artistic failure'.

> And probably more people have thought *Hamlet* a work
> of art because they have found it interesting, than have
> found it interesting because it is a work of art. It is the
> 'Mona Lisa' of literature.[18]

It fails, according to Eliot, because it is doubly a hybrid.
First, as J. M. Robertson claimed in *The Problem of Hamlet*,
the source-play dealt centrally with the theme of revenge,
whereas Shakespeare was more concerned with the effect of
a mother's guilt on her son; and Shakespeare was unable to
reconcile his innovation with the 'intractable' material of
the old play. (This thesis, as we have seen, was later
expanded by Waldock.) Secondly, *Hamlet* is a hybrid in the
sense that the author's darker emotions have sought
expression in the play but, again, have proved incompatible
with the inherited plot. '*Hamlet*, like the sonnets, is full of
some stuff that the writer could not drag to light,
contemplate, or manipulate into art.' (This thesis, in turn,
was to influence L. C. Knights, Derek Traversi and others,
and it partly derives from the notion, widely current around
the turn of the century, that in the period 1600 to 1604
Shakespeare's mind was darkened by morbid and cynical
preoccupations.)
  Eliot then proceeds to his famous formulation of the
'objective correlative':

> The only way of expressing emotion in the form of art is
> by finding an 'objective correlative'; in other words, a set
> of objects, a situation, a chain of events which shall be the
> formula of that *particular* emotion; such that when the
> external facts, which must terminate in sensory
> experience, are given, the emotion is immediately
> evoked.

ıblingly vague, since 'a set of objects, a
ɔf events' include a large number of
ıs; and Eliot's attempts to illustrate the
that it can be interpreted in conflicting
ɛss, he warms to his task of criticising
k from which the objective correlative is,
ʋsly absent. 'Hamlet (the man) is dominated
by an ᴄ. which is inexpressible, because it is in *excess*
of the facts as they appear.' A similar claim will, at the end of
his essay, be made about Shakespeare, and its illogicality
(for if an emotion is inexpressible, we cannot be aware of it)
will there be disguised as a paradox. For the moment, Eliot
glosses over the illogicality by offering an 'explanation'
which markedly alters the claim: 'Hamlet is up against the
difficulty that his disgust is occasioned by his mother, but
that his mother is not an adequate equivalent for it; his
disgust envelops and exceeds her.' In this case, the
emotion—disgust—is expressible and expressed; the
missing objective correlative is an appropriately disgusting
Gertrude. We may wonder whether Eliot would regard
Oedipus Tyrannos as a failure in so far as there is an ironic
disparity between Tiresias's nature and Oedipus's
paranoiac assessment of it.

As if sensing the argument that there may be aptness in
disparity, Eliot proceeds to make an admission which
undermines his main case against *Hamlet* but is presented as
though it constituted clarification and confirmation rather
than self-refutation. He says:

> To have heightened the criminality of Gertrude would
> have been to provide the formula for a totally different
> emotion in Hamlet; it is just *because* her character is so
> negative and insignificant that she arouses in Hamlet the
> feeling which she is incapable of representing.

In other words, there is (after all) a perfectly apt disparity
between Hamlet's vehement disgust and the Gertrude who

is neither vehement nor disgusting. In one of Eliot's senses of the term (utterance vividly appropriate to the speaker's state of mind) the objective correlative is evidently present, while the objective correlative in another sense (an appropriate dramatic context) is provided precisely by its absence in a third sense (a personality which conforms to another character's assessment of that personality). Nevertheless, Eliot, apparently unaware that his main case has lapsed into self-contradiction, concludes his essay by speculating about the 'by hypothesis unknowable' state of mind of Shakespeare which led the author to try to put a quart of emotion into the pint-pot of the play. That a term's definition is spongy may be no impediment to the term's use; indeed, this may facilitate its subsequent popularity: so the 'objective correlative', like Eliot's 'dissociation of sensibility', enjoyed 'a success in the world astonishing to [its] author'.[19]

As we have seen, the contradictions in Eliot's case mean that he is his own best adversary. The 'inexpressible' emotion of Hamlet has been forcefully expressed—it is his disgust at Gertrude; and its 'excess' has also been explained within the essay as appropriate to a Gertrude who does not appear disgusting. The reader could argue, in fact, that Eliot unwittingly provides the basis for a radical defence of *Hamlet*, which is that the play seems consistently concerned to problematise stereotypes and stereotyping. Hamlet seeks to stereotype Gertrude as the lustful widow, but she resists such stereotyping; and there is a similar pattern in his treatment of Ophelia, Polonius and Claudius. Thus *Hamlet* might have a highly sophisticated structure, based on an implicit criticism of Hamlet's endeavour to impose simpler structures upon a complicated reality.

There's a final irony about Eliot's essay which, alas, says much about criticism of *Hamlet* generally. Eliot begins by remarking that critics with creative imaginations 'often find in Hamlet a vicarious existence for their own artistic realization'. So Goethe 'made of Hamlet a Werther', and

Coleridge 'made of Hamlet a Coleridge'. Unfortunately, Eliot failed to draw the obvious conclusion, which is that the creative imagination of T. S. Eliot would make of Hamlet a T. S. Eliot. Yet the connections are obvious. When he was writing that essay, Eliot was struggling to assemble *The Waste Land*; and a central problem for him was to find some means of ordering the whole, of co-ordinating a highly fragmentary work ('These fragments I have shored against my ruins'): so, predictably, he was concerned with the apparent lack of co-ordination in *Hamlet*. In his view, the prince embodies an intense sexual disgust which seems to lack an 'objective correlative': much the same has been said of *The Waste Land*, where the strong misogyny and fascinated loathing for the carnal can seem excessive in a poem which purports to commend sympathy ('Dayadhvam') and not merely 'control'. The '*Hamlet*' essay declares: 'The intense feeling, ecstatic or terrible, without an object or exceeding its object, is something which every person of sensibility has known';[20] and it was certainly a feeling which beset the Eliot of the *Waste Land* period; indeed, subsequently it was to become the basis of *The Family Reunion*, in which Harry is hideously burdened with a sense of guilt which eludes explanation. In short, though J. Alfred Prufrock was not Prince Hamlet, Shakespeare's Hamlet may have served as an 'objective correlative' for T. S. Eliot.

Ernest Jones and William Empson: Oedipus and the Hole

In 1900, in a footnote to *The Interpretation of Dreams*, Sigmund Freud said:

Hamlet is able to do anything—except take vengeance on the man who did away with his father and took that father's place with his mother, the man who shows him the repressed wishes of his own childhood realized.[21]

This idea was seized by Freud's disciple and eventual biographer, Ernest Jones, who developed it extensively over many years: 'The Oedipus Complex as an Explanation of Hamlet's Mystery' appeared in *The American Journal of Psychology*, January 1910; 'A Psycho-Analytic Study of Hamlet' followed as Chapter 1 of Jones's *Essays in Applied Psycho-Analysis* (1923); and *Hamlet and Oedipus* appeared in 1949.

Jones argues that although there is a general consensus that *Hamlet* is an enigma, there is no consensus about the solution to that enigma; nor can it be concluded that there is no solution, since so powerful and fascinating a drama could not be based on vacuity. The solution has been elusive because, hitherto, Sigmund Freud's theory of the Oedipus Complex has not been available to literary critics; now, thanks to Freud (who claimed to be 'empirical' and 'scientific'), the mystery of the play and its protagonist can at last be solved. The reason for Hamlet's delay is that if he killed Claudius he would be killing someone who has fulfilled Hamlet's own repressed Oedipal desires; the destruction of Claudius would resemble the destruction of part of himself.

It is his moral duty, to which his father exhorts him, to put an end to the incestuous activities of his mother (by killing Claudius), but his unconscious does not want to put an end to them (he being identified with Claudius in the situation), and so he cannot. His lashings of self-reproach and remorse are ultimately because of this very failure, i.e. the refusal of his guilty wishes to undo the sin. By refusing to abandon his own incestuous wishes he perpetuates the sin and so must endure the stings of torturing conscience. And yet killing his mother's husband would be equivalent to committing the original

sin himself, which would if anything be even more guilty.
So of the two impossible alternatives he adopts the
passive solution of letting the incest continue vicariously,
but at the same time provoking destruction at the King's
hand. Was ever a tragic figure so torn and tortured![22]

No wonder, then, that Hamlet is attracted by suicide, 'the
least intolerable solution of the problem'. Of course, he
does eventually kill Claudius—but only when Gertrude has
first died and he himself is mortally wounded, thus
eliminating that hideous succuba of incestuous guilt.

The elegance of Jones's account resides in its apparent
ability to explain both large and small matters: his single
notion provides immense transformative power. The delay
has not previously been understood, because critics were
unfamiliar with psycho-analysis; Hamlet cannot understand
his procrastination, because no Freud is available at
Elsinore to enlighten him; his fascinated disgust at
Gertrude's sexuality now becomes fully comprehensible;
and other, lesser peculiarities now fit a pattern. For example,
in *The Murder of Gonzago*, which Hamlet has selected and
adapted for performance, the murderer of the king is not the
brother, as we might expect, but the nephew: which
indicates the way in which, unconsciously, the nephew of
Claudius is intertwined in sexual ambition with the killer of
King Hamlet. Again, on the way to Gertrude's chamber,
Hamlet reflects:

> O heart, lose not thy nature, let not ever
> The soul of Nero enter this firm bosom.
> Let me be cruel, not unnatural.
> I will speak daggers to her, but use none.

Jones comments, 'Nero . . . . . is reputed to have slept with
his mother and then murdered her (presumably for a similar
reason, inability to bear the guilt her continued presence
evoked)' . . .[23]

One objection to Jones's interpretation might be that if Hamlet were so powerfully Oedipal, he would not praise his father so magniloquently; to which the psycho-analyst could answer that Hamlet is guiltily compensating for the Oedipal desire by idealising the father (now that the father is dead) and is directing against Claudius his Oedipal hostility. And with that, the Freudian theory appears no longer empirical. An empirical hypothesis is, by definition, potentially refutable; even when the available evidence consistently supports it, the hypothesis gains probability but can never harden into a certainty; the invidious instance, the awkward bit of contradictory evidence, may arrive at any time. The very comprehensiveness of Jones's interpretation, and the elasticity of its theoretical basis, mean that on its own terms it seems to elude challenge. Since the postulated Oedipus Complex has two aspects (the repressed unconscious desire and the repressing activity of the conscious mind), anything that Hamlet says or does could be regarded as illustrating one or the other: evidence which seems to refute the postulation of the incestuous desire can be used to confirm the postulation of a powerful repression. In short, like Freud himself with his analyses of his patients' symptoms, Jones seems to be arguing on the basis of 'heads I win and tails you lose'. There comes a time when the very comprehensiveness of the Oedipal thesis seems to deny the text its proper instability; and even if Freud were right, the Oedipus Complex would be the common property of millions, while Hamlet remains defiantly unique: no malady entails mercurial intelligence.

The major premise of Jones's theory, the existence of the Oedipus Complex, has been challenged by other reputed experts in psychology, notably Jung and Adler; while Otto Rank has objected that if Hamlet were really in the grip of that incestuous drive, he could have used the injunction of revenge as a pretext to despatch speedily the rival who at present occupies his mother's bed. Another psycho-analyst, Theodore Lidz, claims that the key to the play is less the

Oedipus Complex than the idealisation of the mother:

> *Hamlet* . . . . . does not, in itself, consider the instinctual
> nature of the oedipal situation, or require that Hamlet be
> preoccupied with his hostility to his mother and uncle
> because of a fixation at the oedipal phase of development.
> Rather it deals with what a mother's betrayal of her
> husband can do to a son and with the importance of the
> parents' relationship with each other and to their child
> . . . . . The play primarily stresses the importance of
> continuing intrafamilial relationships to a person's
> emotional stability rather than solely, or primarily, the
> influence of early childhood relationships on later life.[24]

A sceptical reader may reflect that if the significance of
Hamlet lies in its demonstration of 'the importance of
continuing intrafamilial relationships to a person's
emotional stability', Shakespeare has chosen a remarkably
convoluted way of presenting a rather trite doctrine. Indeed,
the reader might well draw from the play a very different
lesson: *Hamlet* shows that the disruption of 'intrafamilial
relationships' may liberate intensities of experience and
insight which call in question the value of stable, secure and
distinctly un-tragic existence. If Shakespeare wished to
impart readily-summarisable messages to the world, he
would have become a priest or a pamphleteer and not a
dramatist. Nevertheless, during the twentieth century the
psycho-analytic quest for the stiff key to the lock of *Hamlet*,
the struggle to decipher a coded message, continued
indefatigably; and eventually Jacques Lacan was pleased to
declare that the ghost which haunts the play is really the
phallus:

> The very source of what makes Hamlet's arm waver at
> every moment, is the narcissistic connection that Freud
> tells us about in his text on the decline of the Oedipus

complex: one cannot strike the phallus, because the phallus, even the real phallus, is a *ghost*.[25]

Nevertheless, while Lacan saw a play dominated by the phallic ghost, another critic had seen a play whose centre was a gaping hole.

The resilient theory that Hamlet's delay should be explained on technical rather than on psychological grounds received new vigour from William Empson's essay '*Hamlet* When New' (1953). Empson begins with a number of speculative assumptions: Shakespeare was asked by his company to revise and bring up to date an earlier *Hamlet*, written by Thomas Kyd in the 1580s. The old *Hamlet* would have seemed impressively stately to its original audiences; but now, more than a decade later, it would seem too slow, and the spectators would feel like shouting 'Hurry up!' at the hero. So, Shakespeare thought:

'The only way to shut this hole is to make it big. I shall make Hamlet walk up to the audience and tell them, again and again, "I don't know why I'm delaying any more than you do; the motivation of this play is just as blank to me as it is to you; but I can't help it." What is more, I shall make it impossible for them to blame him. And *then* they daren't laugh.' [26]

This method, says Empson, 'instead of reducing the old play to farce, made it thrillingly life-like and profound'. To keep speculation alive, Shakespeare incorporated plenty of interesting topical material: melancholy was a fashionable malaise, so Hamlet exhibits it; vacillation was a notorious characteristic not only of the Earl of Essex but even of Queen Elizabeth, so Hamlet vacillates conspicuously. Puritanical diatribes against women and luxury were included; the ethics of revenge were exposed for questioning; and, throughout, an intriguing friction between realism and theatricality was generated: 'Hamlet

. . . . . walks out to the audience and says "You think this an absurd old play, and so it is, *but I'm in it*, and what can I do?" [27] In short, Shakespeare succeeded in revitalising the original *Hamlet* by turning the hero's character into a 'baffling mystery'. There was plenty to fascinate and intrigue the audiences, plenty to make them argue and speculate; but the mystery has merely an external explanation and not an internal solution: at the centre of Hamlet (and *Hamlet*) is a large, conspicuous and attractively-rimmed hole.

Empson's essay is engagingly lively; its weakness is the speculative basis. The earlier *Hamlet* may well have seemed, by 1600, the cumbrous, dated, plodding piece that Empson envisages, but it isn't available for inspection. If delay were a prominent mystery in that *Ur-Hamlet*, much of his case would dissolve. Again, Empson makes generous assumptions about the Elizabethan audience's response to Shakespeare's play; but, apart from the brief notes that *Hamlet* is able to 'please the wiser sort' and indeed 'please all', we have remarkably little evidence of the audience response, and certainly no proof that the patrons left the theatre in a state of excited and argumentative bafflement. Empson's *Hamlet* sounds like a play to delight Pirandello; yet, though there are Pirandellian glimpses in a few of Shakespeare's scenes, the earth and flagstones of Elsinore are usually too solid beneath the feet, and the skulls too prominent in that earth, for Hamlet to be recruited by *Six Characters in Search of an Author*. Nevertheless, the prince who describes the ghost as 'this fellow in the cellarage' is surely winking conspiratorially in the direction of William Empson.

Marxist and Deconstructionist Versions

Many people have claimed to be Marxists; the one person with the authority to adjudicate their claims, Karl Marx, is no longer in a position to do so, having joined the silent majority (the dead) in 1883. Critics who deem themselves to be Marxists have adopted conflicting approaches (formalism, socialist realism, structuralism, post-structuralism, etc.) and have been assailed by other critics who purport to be Marxists. One of the contradictions in Marx's theories is that his view of literature is both reductive and enhancive. When the *Communist Manifesto* says that the poet is merely one of the 'paid wage-labourers' of 'the bourgeoisie' and remarks that 'Your very ideas are but the outgrowth of the conditions of your bourgeois production and bourgeois property', this encourages the view that literature is merely a vehicle of ideological propaganda rather than of truth and insight; yet Marx himself, in his passionate love of literature (particularly of Shakespeare's works) and by his habit of using literary quotations and allusions to support his arguments, repeatedly celebrated the cognitive, truth-seeking and epitomising power of creative writing.

By now there is a consensus that the leading Marxist dramatist of the twentieth century is Bertolt Brecht (even if the extent of his commitment to Marxism is still a matter of debate). Brecht has been acclaimed for his theatrical innovations, particularly the so-called 'Alienation Effects' or *Verfremdungseffekten*; but his theoretical writings, notably *The Messingkauf Dialogues*, make clear that he saw himself as a traditionalist, in the sense that he was attempting to restore to the theatre its former vitality—above all the healthily profane vitality of the Elizabethan playhouse: 'A theatre full of A-effects!' This nostalgic enthusiasm is evident when the speakers in *The Messingkauf Dialogues* turn to *Hamlet*:

The Dramaturg: The star of Shakespeare's Globe Theatre . . . . . was a stout man and short of breath, and so for a while all the heroes had to be stout and short of breath . . . . . As a result the plot was deepened for him; and probably by him, too. Cascades and rapids were built in. The play became so much more interesting; it looks as if

they must have remodelled and readapted it on the stage
as far as Act IV, then found themselves faced with the
problem of how to bring this hesitant Hamlet up to the
final ranting bloodbath that was the hit scene of the
original play. Act IV contains a number of scenes each of
which represents one possible solution. The actor may
have needed to use the whole lot; or perhaps he only
needed one, and the rest were none the less included in
the book . . . . .

The Actor: From what you've said I'd picture Shakespeare
coming along with a fresh scene every day.

The Dramaturg: Exactly. I feel they were experimenting.
They were experimenting just as Galileo was
experimenting in Florence at that time and Bacon in
London. And so it is right to stage the plays in a spirit of
experiment . . . . .

The Philosopher: Hamlet's new bourgeois way of thinking
is part of Hamlet's sickness. His experiments lead straight
to disaster . . . . . All right; zigzag. In a sense the play has
the permanence of something makeshift . . . . .[28]

Brecht's sense of Hamlet's 'new bourgeois way of
thinking' tallies with the account of Shakespeare given by
the English Marxist, Christopher Caudwell, in *Illusion and
Reality* (1937):

Marlowe, Chapman, Greene, but above all Shakespeare,
born of bourgeois parents, exactly express the cyclonic
force of the princely bourgeois will in this era, in all its
vigour and recklessness. Lear, Hamlet, Macbeth,
Antony, Troilus, Othello, Romeo and Coriolanus, each
in his different way knows no other obligation than to be
the thing he is, to realise himself to the last drop, to give
out in its purest and most exquisite form the aroma of
self . . . . .

The depth with which Shakespeare moved in the
bourgeois illusion, the greatness of his grasp of human

society, is shown by the fact that he is ultimately a tragedian. This unfettered realism of human individualities involves for him the equally unfettered play of Necessity. The contradiction which is the driving force of capitalism finds its expression again and again in Shakespeare's tragedies.[29]

For a later Marxist, Terry Eagleton (in *William Shakespeare*, 1986), Hamlet does not have a 'new bourgeois way of thinking' at all:

His 'self' consists simply in the range of gestures with which he resists available definitions, not in a radical alternative beyond their reach. It is thus wholly parasitic on the positions it refuses . . . . .

Eagleton's Hamlet is caught between two worlds and belongs to neither:

Hamlet is a radically transitional figure, strung out between a traditional social order to which he is marginal, and a future epoch of achieved bourgeois individualism which will surpass it. But because of this we can glimpse in him a negative critique of the forms of subjectivity typical of *both* these regimes . . . . . What it is to be a subject, in short, is a political problem for Hamlet, as it has once more become a political problem for us.[30]

Hence his modernity: we have become critical, with hindsight, of the modes of selfhood permitted by the bourgeois era; Hamlet, by his 'decentred' identity, has questioned bourgeois individualism in advance; he is proleptic, we are analeptic. Thus Eagleton's view exemplifies the general rule that a critic who values a text will usually discover that it astutely endorses his or her prejudices.

In the 1960s and 1970s, post-structuralism and

deconstructionism gave new life to some old Romantic notions. Blake and Shelley had emphasised that human nature is largely a construct and that individuals are, to a far greater extent than they wish to admit, 'authored' and 'authorised' by the authorities of the state; revolutionise society and you could revolutionise human nature. This notion contributes to Eagleton's enthusiasm for his centrally 'hollow' Hamlet. Another Romantic preoccupation which was rejuvenated in the period 1965–85 was the interest in radical contradiction: Blake's 'Without Contraries is no progression' and 'Milton . . . . . was a true poet and of the devil's party without knowing it' contain the gist of much of the twentieth century's more radical literary theory. The quest for contraries and paradox was displayed in Terence Hawkes's essay, '*Telmah*' (1985). Hawkes argues that within *Hamlet* we can discern *Hamlet reversed*— *Telmah*—when we perceive that Claudius is no simple villain but Hamlet's 'mighty opposite', 'and that mightiness constantly tugs back, recursively, against the smooth flow of a play that bears, perhaps surprisingly, only the prince's name'. Hence, *Telmah* is 'a sense of an everpresent potential challenge and contradiction *within* and *implied by* the text that we name *Hamlet*'. Hawkes then commends a familiar but useful cliché of literary theorists in the 1980s, the claim that a text should be regarded as 'a site of struggle':

> I propose: the sense of the text as a site, or an area of conflicting and often contradictory potential interpretations, no single one or group of which can claim 'intrinsic' primacy or 'inherent' authority, and all of which are always ideological in nature and subject to extrinsic political and economic determinants.[31]

The reader may notice that Hawkes's proposal is weakened by the implication that it, too, is 'ideological in nature' and can therefore claim no 'intrinsic' primacy or 'inherent' authority. In the past, critics often overvalued textual unity and harmony; in the late twentieth century, critics often overvalued textual disunity and discord. *Hamlet* beckons and derides both these traditions of simplification.

A SUMMARY

When we look back over that selection of critical interpretations, we see that for centuries *Hamlet* has offered provocation and defiance to its interpreters. The enigma of *Hamlet* seems to have grown with ever-increasing energy; indeed, it appears to grow in proportion to the enigma-solving energies expended it upon it. There is a symbiotic relationship between the play's power to question and the critical power expended on possible answers. *Hamlet* asks many questions; what has lent them such recalcitrant vigour is largely the zealous hubris of the critical industry and even of what might be termed intellectual imperialism. Whole armies of pen-wielders have advanced into *Hamlet's* ambush; the soldiers fall, and *Hamlet* continues its advance, gorged on the fallen and reinvigorated by them.

Hamlet has been called the Sphynx of modern literature.[32] The legendary Sphynx which terrified ancient Thebes crouched by the roadside and set the same riddle to each quester: 'What is it that goes on four legs in the morning, two legs at noon, and three legs in the evening?' The questers repeatedly failed to solve it, and were then destroyed by the Sphynx. The irony was that the answer was already there, exemplified by each of the victims; the answer being 'Man'. Similarly, *Hamlet* says to each quester: 'What is the solution to the riddle of my meaning? Is it psychological, or ethical, or technical? Or would you care to venture the "solution" that the riddle is insoluble?' And every quester replies, and is defeated. Yet each exemplifies at least one answer: 'The paradox of rationality, which (contesting meanings) converts an apparent solution into the basis of a new problem.'

Many commentators on *Hamlet* have assumed that there
should be an interpretation which will render the whole play
coherent and rational; they seek to close what the text leaves
open, to complete a narrative the text leaves incomplete, to
smooth what is rough. Other commentators, having
unsuccessfully attempted this operation, may declare that
the text is irredeemably muddled: no solution can be found.
The former group is rebuked by the inadequacy of a
'unitary' explanation to master the disunities of the play; the
second group is rebuked by the persistent refusal of other
critics to take 'no solution' as an answer; if there is no
consensus about a solution, there is no consensus that there
is no solution. Commentators who purport to welcome a
free plurality of interpretations soon deem some
interpretations to be less welcome than others. Repeatedly
the play exposes the ideological egotism of its critics: it
fragments a 'Marxist' approach into the conflicting notions
of self-styled Marxists, and it fragments a
'deconstructionist' approach into the conflicting notions of
purported deconstructionists. To call the text 'a site of
struggle' is perhaps to use a melodramatic term for the
obvious: the value of a good literary work lies in its
renewable excess: the interpretations will always be
exceeded by the text's potential meanings, which are
clarified yet adulterated by rational discourse. A joke
explained won't make you laugh, a lamentation analysed
won't make you weep; and the play's fusions of thought and
feeling, of abstract and concrete, of the ethical and the
aesthetic, have a value which rightly provokes yet inevitably
outdistances the reach of rational expository prose. *Hamlet*
makes this traditional problem more acute by putting a
passionately enquiring intellectual at the centre of an
unconventionally ambiguous drama, and by showing that a
flawed and unfinished script can be an excellent basis for a
theatrically vital play.

·1·
Hamlet Unbrac'd:
Problems, Gaps, Anomalies

If we summon up Hamlet's image on the screen of memory
and imagination, we are likely to see a handsome, brooding,
meditative young man, perhaps dressed in an 'inky cloak'
and suit of 'solemn black'; he looks, at any rate, thoughtful,
and his appearance is at least unembarrassing. We are less
likely to recall a distinctly embarrassing spectacle:

> Lord Hamlet, with his doublet all unbrac'd,
> No hat upon his head, his stockings foul'd,
> Ungarter'd and down-gyvèd to his ankle,
> Pale as his shirt, his knees knocking each other . . . . .[1]

This is the dishevelled, dirty Hamlet who appears to
Ophelia, his inner disorder expressed with almost ludicrous
overtness in his sartorial disarray. Yet this grotesquely
undignified Hamlet stands as a mute reproach to those who
would tidy and smooth both his character and the play as a
whole. An interpretation of *Hamlet* which ignores its
embarrassing, awkward, recalcitrant features is a
falsification. So, in this part of the book, I deliberately
emphasise the problems, gaps and anomalies of the text, and
some related problems of its context. *Hamlet* is in various
ways a looser, freer text than we tend to assume. A doublet
unbrac'd (unbuttoned, perhaps flapping open) is untidy but

1

may give the wearer more freedom to breathe; *Hamlet*
unbrac'd may put more breathing-space and flexibility into
our responses.

SOURCES

Hamlet is a major, distinctive and characteristic work of
Shakespeare's; yet a survey of the known sources soon
reveals that in large and small matters it is indebted to tales,
legends and sagas extending back into the mists of time. To
compare is to contrast; the more we notice these debts to
tradition, the more we see what is distinctive about
Shakespeare's adaptation and regeneration of the old
materials. Fortunately and unfortunately, there is a 'Missing
Link' in the transmission: we lack the so-called *Ur-Hamlet*,
the Hamlet play whose author was almost certainly Thomas
Kyd. It is fortunate, in the sense that such a known gap in the
sequence alerts us to the possibility of unknown gaps elsewhere; we are reminded that the survival of texts from the
Elizabethan period has been a hazardous matter, and, if more
texts had survived, our understanding of Shakespeare and
other major authors would inevitably be enhanced. But predominantly the loss of the *Ur-Hamlet* is unfortunate. That
work represented a crucial phase in the transmission, the
phase during which a prose narrative was converted into a
verse drama. We are so near and yet so far, because Kyd's
Spanish Tragedy has survived, and that play contains enough
similarities to Shakespeare's *Hamlet* to compel speculation
about the content of the *Ur-Hamlet*. This speculation has
sometimes been so confident and detailed as to give the
impression that the *Ur-Hamlet* is a thinly-veiled presence
rather than an absence; but absent it remains, and, were it to
come to light at last, it might well surprise the speculators.
    Earlier we noted that one persistent critical argument
(offered by Robertson, Waldock and Eliot, among others) is
that the problems of *Hamlet* result from a tension or even

contradiction between Shakespeare's interests and the source materials. I claim in this book that *Hamlet* is both looser and tighter than is often recognised. Looser, in that by accident and design it is freer, more mobile and pliable, more 'incomplete' than most of us initially suppose; 'tighter' in that, in addition to an extensive co-ordinating thematic and ironic network, the play has deliberate lacunae, 'digressions' and puzzles: it has a central interrogative principle. A survey of the early sources of the play emphasises the palimpsestic or mongrelly qualities of both *Hamlet* and its hero, and may at first seem to support the theory that there is a conflict between Shakespeare's inclinations and the inherited legend. On the other hand, when we take account not only of the Hamlet tradition but also of interests which Shakespeare was pursuing in various plays of his prior to *Hamlet*, we may find that there is evidence to support the case for extensive intentional co-ordination in *Hamlet*—not the kind which projects clear answers but the kind which deliberately generates the possibility of layered alternative readings. Gradually we should see that the play is characterised by a fruitful friction between muddle and complexity, the improvised and the orchestrated, the traditional and the innovatory.

The Tradition of the Crazy Avenger

The Latin word *brutus* means 'heavy, dull or stupid'. Hamlet puns partly on this when Polonius remarks that while enacting Julius Caesar he was slain by Brutus: Hamlet responds, 'it was a brute part of him . . . . .' An earlier, less historical and more legendary Brutus than the assassin of Caesar was Lucius Junius. After the murder of his elder brother by an uncle, Lucius eluded a similar fate by pretending to be an idiot, thus gaining the nickname 'Brutus'. When chaste Lucretia was raped by Tarquin and subsequently slew herself, this Brutus abandoned the pretence of stupidity and led the Roman people to expel the royal Tarquins and to establish a republic in Rome. Shakespeare's *The Rape of Lucrece* says of his emergence:

> He with the Romans was esteemèd so
>> As silly jeering idiots are with kings,
>> For sportive words and utt'ring foolish things.

> But now he throws that shallow habit by
>> Wherein deep policy did him disguise,
>> And arm'd his long-hid wits advisedly . . . . . [2]

The Roman emperor Claudius, too, feigned stupidity as a protective device in perilous times; the biblical David 'feigned himself mad' when he was afraid of Achish, King of Gath (I Samuel 21: 10–15); and, in any case, ancient folk-tales, legends and sagas contain numerous embodiments of the theme of the wise fool, cunning idiot or apparently-deranged seer, from Trojan Cassandra and the Sybils who prophesy in a state of frenzy or dementia, to the riddling gnomes and crones of fairy-tales.

An obvious but neglected irony of Shakespeare's *Hamlet* is that the name of its sophisticated and intellectual protagonist is, etymologically, Dimwit. (*Amloði*, Old Norse for 'dimwitted'.) The 'wise fool' called Amloði, Amlotha or Amleth emerges from medieval Icelandic sagas into the *Historiae Danicae* of the Dane, Saxo Grammaticus. Saxo's history was written at the end of the twelfth century and was first printed in 1514. Amleth is one of several figures in the *Historiae Danicae* who feign insanity in order to preserve themselves while planning revenge: these include Uffe, Harald and Halfden. Saxo tells how Horwendil, King of Jutland, killed the King of Norway in single combat; subsequently he married Gerutha, who bore Amleth. Horwendil was then treacherously murdered by his envious brother, Feng (or Fengon); and Feng 'took the wife of the brother he had butchered, capping unnatural murder wth incest'. He allayed hostility by claiming that he had killed Horwendil to save Gerutha from his cruelty. Amleth perceived the truth, but feared that his uncle might suspect him; 'So he chose to feign dulness, and pretend an utter lack of wits. This cunning course not only concealed his intelligence but ensured his safety.' Furthermore, he smeared himself with filth and became listless and lethargic. Yet, oddly enough, the guise of idiocy which was intended to avert suspicion had the natural consequence of arousing it—particularly when he prepared barbed rods and said he would use them to avenge his father. As a test, courtiers then arranged for a young woman who had been his childhood companion to waylay him, the courtiers reasoning that if Amleth proceeds to copulate with her, he's no fool. He does indeed copulate with her, but persuades her to say that nothing of the kind has happened; and her story is believed. A further test is then devised: a courtier hides beneath a straw mattress in Gerutha's chamber in order to eavesdrop on Amleth's private conversation with her.

Afraid of being overheard by some eavesdropper, [Amleth] at first resorted to his usual imbecile ways, and crowed like a noisy cock, beating his arms together to mimic the flapping of wings. Then he mounted the straw and began to swing his body and jump again and again, wishing to try if aught lurked there in hiding. Feeling a lump beneath his feet, he drove his sword into the spot, and impaled him who lay hid. Then he dragged him from his concealment and slew him. Then, cutting his body into morsels, he seethed it in boiling water, and flung it through the mouth of an open sewer for the swine to eat, bestrewing the stinking mire with his hapless limbs. Having in this wise eluded the snare, he went back to the room. Then his mother set up a great wailing, and began to lament her son's folly to his face; but he said: 'Most infamous of women! dost thou seek with such lying lamentations to hide thy most heavy guilt? Wantoning like a harlot, thou hast entered a wicked and abominable state of wedlock, embracing with incestuous bosom thy husband's slayer, and wheedling with filthy lures of blandishments him who had slain the father of thy son. This, forsooth, is the way that the mares couple with the vanquishers of their mates; for brute beasts are naturally incited to pair indiscriminately . . . . .[3]

He then explains that his madness is a guise, that he seeks to avenge his father's death, and that Gerutha should 'keep silence'.

Amleth jests callously about the eavesdropper's death, and consequently Feng determines to have Amleth killed—not in Jutland, where Gerutha would be distressed, but in Britain. So Amleth is sent to Britain with two envoys who bear a letter enjoining the British king to carry out the killing. On the journey, Amleth finds the letter and alters it so that it becomes not only a death-warrant for the hapless envoys but also a petition for his marriage to the British king's daughter; the envoys are executed, and Amleth marries the princess. He returns to Jutland, where his own supposed death is being celebrated, makes the courtiers drunk, binds them, and finally murders them by setting fire to the palace; he seeks out Feng and, having first exchanged swords so that Feng·wields a useless one (nailed into its scabbard), slays him. Saxo comments:

O valiant Amleth, and worthy of immortal fame, who being shrewdly armed with a feint of folly, covered a wisdom too high for human wit under a marvellous disguise of silliness! and not only found in his subtlety means to protect his own safety, but also by its guidance found opportunity to avenge his father. By his skilful defence of himself, and strenuous revenge for his parent, he has left it doubtful whether we are to think more of his wit or his bravery.[4]

After the slaughter at the palace, Amleth makes a long oration to the people, contrasting the usurper Feng with the admirable Horwendil, and is accepted as rightful king. In subsequent adventures, he gains a second wife (Hermutrude, Queen of Scotland), kills the treacherous British king and plunders his lands, and is eventually slain in battle by Wiglek of Denmark. His widow Hermutrude then readily becomes the 'spoil and bride' of the victor: at which the chronicler, Saxo, utters a diatribe against the fickleness and lustfulness of women.

It is possible that Shakespeare had direct knowledge of Saxo's *Historiae Danicae*, but this seems unlikely; there is a greater likelihood that he knew directly François de Belleforest's version of Saxo. Belleforest's *Histoires Tragiques*, published between 1559 and 1582, provided a storehouse of material for English writers, and it probably contributed, directly or indirectly, to Shakespeare's *Rape of Lucrece, Romeo and Juliet, Much Ado About Nothing* and *Twelfth Night*. Belleforest follows the main story of Amleth as given by Saxo; he reduces the more archaic, folklorish elements (e.g. the exposition of the hero's gnomic riddles) and adds a considerable amount of moralistic commentary, emphasising the difference between the relatively brutal pre-Christian times he is describing and the more enlightened age for which he is writing. He expands the misogynistic material, and changes the story to make Gerutha a willing adulteress with Feng before the murder of her first husband. A brief parenthesis notes that 'over great drinking' is 'a vice common and familiar among the Almaines, and other nations inhabiting the north parts of the world', and the ethics of revenge are considered at some length, Belleforest finding warrant for it in the Bible (notably I Kings 2: 5–6, 8–9).[5]

Around 1589 the story of Amleth was adapted as the English play which scholars now call 'the *Ur-Hamlet*'. A satiric passage by Thomas Nashe strongly indicates that the playwright was Kyd. Harold Jenkins claims: 'It is as inconceivable that the *Ur-Hamlet* did not use Belleforest as it is that Shakespeare did not use the *Ur-Hamlet*. He cánnot have been unfamiliar with a play which was acted at the Theatre and which probably therefore belonged to his own company.'[6] By 1596 Thomas Lodge (in *Wits Miserie*) could refer scornfully to the pallid ghost 'which cried so miserally at the Theator like an oister wife, *Hamlet, reuenge*'.[7] Kyd's *Spanish Tragedy* indicates that the *Ur-Hamlet* contained long rhetorical speeches of lamentation and melancholy from the central character, an avenging Hamlet who, if he resembled the vengeful Hieronymo, would have veered between sanity and madness; and the prominence of the play-within-the-play in *The Spanish Tragedy* encourages the view that there was a kindred device in the *Ur-Hamlet*.

If we now consider the elements of Shakespeare's *Hamlet* which evidently derive (in one way or another but probably via the *Ur-Hamlet*) from Saxo and Belleforest, this list emerges:

1. The murder of a king by his brother, who succeeds to the throne and incestuously marries the widowed queen.
2. The association of a funeral with revelry and drunkenness.
3. Denunciation of drunkenness as a disreputable national custom.
4. Revenge is planned by the son of the murdered king.
5. The son behaves in a manner which seems deranged or foolish and which has the effect of arousing suspicion instead of averting it.
6. In his melancholy, the son appears in a dirty and dishevelled state.
7. Attempts are made to test and penetrate his guise of derangement. In one, an attractive young woman is used as 'bait'; in another, a courtier who is concealed in the queen's chamber is discovered and killed by the hero, and the corpse is disposed of in a rough and base way.

8. Her son, in private, upbraids the queen at length for her lustful infidelity to her late husband, assures her that he is not really mad, and enjoins her to keep his secret.

9. Women generally are denounced as lustful and fickle.

10. The usurper decides that the hero is so dangerous that he must be slain; he also decides, however, that the slaying should take place not in Scandinavia but in Britain. The hero is sent by sea with two courtiers who bear a letter asking the British king to effect the execution; the hero secretly alters the letter so that the two courtiers unwittingly bear their own death-warrant and accordingly perish.

11. The hero returns to his homeland at a time of funeral.

12. The hero slays the usurping king by means of a sword after an exchange of swords (one of which has been tampered with).

We can also add a list of items which, with varying degrees of probability, derive from the *Ur-Hamlet* and/or from *The Spanish Tragedy* (*ST*):

1. A ghost enjoins revenge. (Reported of the *Ur-Hamlet*; present in *The Spanish Tragedy*.)

2. The hero, distrusting an injunction to revenge which identifies the evil-doer, seeks independent corroboration of the indictment. (*ST*, III.ii. 24–52; III.vii. 34–54.)[8]

3. The hero reproaches himself for the delay in vengeance and is also reproached for it by another character. (*ST*, III.vii. 69–70; III.ix. 7–8; III.xiii. 95–107; IV.i. 1–29; IV.ii. 29–34. In Kyd, one ostensible reason for delay—barred access to the king—appears so implausible as to indicate that the true explanation is the dramatist's desire to prolong the play.)

4. The hero contemplates suicide. (*ST*, II.v. 67–80; III.xii. 1–19.)

5. There occurs the derangement and self-inflicted death of a grief-stricken bereaved woman. (*ST*, IV.ii. 1–38.)

6. The tears of another person remind the hero of his own cause for grief. (*ST*, III.xiii. 83–5, 95–107; III.xiii. 160–68.)

7. The hero's revenge is furthered by means of a modified play which he has arranged to have performed at court; its plot epitomises part of the main action. (*ST*, IV.iv. 11–152.)

8. The hero dies soon after achieving his revenge. (This happens in *ST* and is in any case a familiar convention in Elizabethan revenge drama.)

The conversion of a loose, episodic prose narrative into a poetic drama for the commercial theatre will have entailed many changes. To be practical, the playwright of the *Ur-Hamlet* would have had to reduce the time-scale and geographical range of the original, simultaneously reducing the number of characters to a manageable group of figures. Matter extraneous to the central issue of revenge (e.g. Amleth's two marriages) would probably have been eliminated.

There is another body of source-material which contributes to *Hamlet*, sometimes with the effect of intensifying the Amleth material, sometimes with the effect of transforming it. This source-material is provided by the imaginative explorations that Shakespeare made in his previous plays. Particularly important, and neglected by commentators, are the connections between the second tetralogy of history plays (*Richard II*, *1 Henry IV*, *2 Henry IV* and *Henry V*) and *Hamlet*.

The characterisation of Prince Hal in that tetralogy is complex and open to divergent interpretations. He is capable of pranks, jesting and buffoonery, but also of ruthless action; he is introspective and self-analytic. His waywardness, in spending his time not at court but at the tavern with Falstaff and his companions, he justifies to himself as a strategy; not only is he getting to know the people of the kingdom he will one day rule, but also his eventual emergence into the realm of princely responsibility will seem the more impressive by contrast with his supposed former irresponsibility. Yet this can be seen as the rationalisation of a procrastinator, of someone who, in spending time with Falstaff and his crew, is actually seeking (by engaging in wayward pleasure) to postpone the time when he must eventually bear heavy political responsibilities. He gains the mantle of martial honour by vanquishing Hotspur in battle, even though he has been shrewdly capable of seeing Hotspur's code of martial honour as a kind of adolescent immaturity; and when eventually he becomes king, he is bitterly and even guiltily aware of his burden of responsibility, and displays a consistent tendency to lay on others the blame for his harsher decisions. In Henry VI, Richard II, Henry IV and particularly in Hal, Shakespeare displays a conflict between the royal role and the actor, between the responsibility imposed and the private individual suffering under the burden. Hamlet can be seen as the culmination of this interest in the divided prince. There is a further, and structurally very important, connection between Hamlet and that second tetralogy. If we compare Hamlet with the source-tale in Saxo and Belleforest, we see that Hamlet is much more familial: the action is largely co-ordinated by connections, parallelisms and contrasts between intermingled families. And this was a principle used throughout that second tetralogy. To take just one instance: Shakespeare (in defiance of historical fact) makes Harry Monmouth and Harry Hotspur coevals; both are young rivals for the throne, sons of rebellious fathers who are now ageing and ailing, and they are frequently compared with each other. Furthermore, Hal (Harry Monmouth) is compared by his father with the young Richard, while Hotspur is compared with the young Bolingbroke; and Hal (who, like Hamlet, rejoices in play-acting) proves to be a skilful mimic of Hotspur. This principle appears to be one

of the most distinctive additions made by Shakespeare to
the Amleth legend: Laertes now appears as a rival to Hamlet,
both young men being avengers of slain fathers, both being
contenders for the throne; rivals even in swordsmanship
and funerary rhetoric. In *Titus Andronicus* Shakespeare had
established a contrast between, on the one hand, the
reluctant 'just' avenger and, on the other, the cunning
Machiavellian avenger and the choleric hasty avenger; and
this contrast echoes mutedly in 1 and 2 *Henry IV* and
burgeons in *Hamlet*. A related theme of various plays, and
one which becomes particularly prominent in *Julius Caesar*
and *Hamlet*, is the recognition that bloody action, even if in
an 'honourable' cause, is likely to blight the agent and harm
the innocent: the hesitations of Brutus anticipate the
vacillations of Hamlet.

Another recurrent figure is the king who has gained the
throne by usurpation and the killing of the legitimate
monarch, and who suffers pangs of conscience but cannot
bring himself to atone for the deed by relinquishing the
throne: Henry IV and Henry V are, in this respect, relatives
of Claudius, and all differ thus from the remorseless Feng of
the Amleth saga. Shakespeare's tetralogy from *Richard II* to
Henry V confirms the impression established starkly by the
nightmarish   revenge-drama,   *Titus   Andronicus*:   that
Shakespeare has an unconventionally vivid sense of the
traditional interconnections between the different meanings
of the key-term 'appetite'. This is a key-term because it
connotes not only alimentary voracity (drunkenness,
gluttony) but also sexual lust and selfish political ambition.
Claudius, as an incestuous usurper and patron of drunken
festivity, exemplifies the continuing force of the 'appetite-
nexus'   in   Shakespeare's   imagination.   Some   of
Shakespeare's later sonnets, and parts of *Love's Labour's
Lost*, show that what elsewhere might seem a conventional
misogyny could be heightened by Shakespeare into a
peculiarly intense rendering of sexual disgust; indeed,
Eliot's theory that in *Hamlet* this disgust is disproportionate

to its dramatic context derives some support from the fact that in *Love's Labour's Lost*, Berowne's bitter self-reproaches at his attraction to Rosaline seem more appropriate to one infatuated by the immoral 'dark lady' of the sonnets than to someone enamoured of the virtuous Rosaline whom we see.

The 'play within the play' in *Hamlet* may derive from Kyd (either from *Ur-Hamlet* or *The Spanish Tragedy* or both), but in *Titus Andronicus, The Taming of the Shrew, Love's Labour's Lost* and *A Midsummer Night's Dream* we see Shakespeare pursuing his interest in the possibilities of an 'inner' drama ironically related to an 'outer' drama (the situations of one being echoed or intensified in the other); in tests of character provided by actors and acting; and in metaphoric relationships between fiction and reality. The original Amleth was an actor (when he feigned idiocy), but Saxo was little interested in the philosophical implications of such feigning. In *Hamlet*, on the other hand, one of the subtlest co-ordinating features is a massive implicit pun on the verb 'to act', which can mean 'to be active in the real world' (as in completing a task of revenge) *or* something very different: 'to play-act, to enter the world of fictional appearances'. Another thematic preoccupation in *Hamlet* is with death as leveller, particularly the leveller of the high and mighty. Although this theme is ancient and traditional, Shakespeare had given it new eloquence not only in his sonnets but also in *Richard II* and 2 *Henry IV*. Lastly, and very important, is the fact that since his early days as a dramatist, Shakespeare had gradually been exploring the possibilities of realism in dialogue and characterisation, and this exploration was often closely related to the exposition of cynical or sceptical ideas. (By the time of *Hamlet*, furthermore, Shakespeare may well have had access to the intricately sceptical relativism of Montaigne.)

If we now look back over this wide range of source-materials and Shakespearian preoccupations, we see a series of interlinked paradoxes. In the case of Saxo's chronicle, we find that one of the most remarkable aspects is that, although the saga of Amleth was written in the twelfth century and clearly has its origins in pre-Christian Scandinavian legends and folk-tales, an astonishing number of its features have survived, many centuries later, in Shakespeare's *Hamlet*. Even details like Hamlet's appearance before Ophelia with 'stockings foul'd' or the exchange of rapiers have clear though variant precedent in Saxo. Thus some features of the traditional story can provide one type of explanation of some of the more problematic features in *Hamlet*. Commentators who argue that Hamlet is by nature too sensitive for the task of revenge (hence his delay) have to contend with the facts that Hamlet despatches Polonius, displaying little remorse, and that he sends Rosencrantz and Guildenstern to their deaths with an ingenuity that he seems to find exhilarating. In each case the treatment of the victims seems harsher than they deserve, and Hamlet's lack of compunction may appear difficult to reconcile with the kind and scrupulous behaviour that he is capable of displaying elsewhere (notably in his magnanimity to Horatio and the players). It can then be argued that Shakespeare's Hamlet encompasses both modern and archaic experience: some of his actions derive from a more primitive, brutal and ruthless literary forebear, and the result is a character who is not the ancient Amleth nor the modern Hamlet but a hybrid who could be called Hamleth. Against that view, the elements of psychological realism in Shakespeare's play, the character's introspective searchings, and the complex comparative network that Shakespeare has developed, all may encourage a reader who seeks a psychological type of unifying explanation: to this reader, Hamlet may appear manic-depressive in temperament, now melancholy and lethargic, now capable of bursts of energy and glee.

Again, it can be argued that the Amleth tradition also explains why Hamlet, even though he has recently resolved to kill Claudius, so readily agrees to travel to England with Rosencrantz and Guildenstern. His 'motive' is literary and external: he yields to the pressure of legend which says 'This is what you traditionally do'. But an alternative scansion, the psychological, can readily postulate yet another rationalisation of delay by Hamlet: the prince has an inner reluctance to kill Claudius (perhaps because of an Oedipus Complex or some ethical misgivings) and therefore embarks on a procrastinative voyage. As for the celebrated mystery of Hamlet's feigned madness and its extent: this too can be explained as source-generated, a yielding to the pressure of the Amleth legend and of many ancient traditions (partly biblical, partly classical, partly from folklore) of the wise fool, shrewd buffoon or deranged seer. As we have seen, the feigned madness is ineffectual as a protective disguise, since it attracts suspicion: it had done so even in Saxo's version. This suggests that even Saxo's hero was not a unified character but a palimpsest, a muddle of old and new. When Amleth, in the queen's chamber, crows like a cockerel while flapping his arms as if they were wings (behaviour superfluous for the purpose of detecting the eavesdropper—he could simply have conducted a normal search), we sense that into a twelfth-century narrative intrudes some far more primitive (totemic or shamanistic) material concerning the desire of men to learn from the animal kingdom and acquire its powers by imitative propitiation. Yet, once again, Shakespeare's *Hamlet* provides the leverage for anyone who wishes to offer a psychological explanation of the feigned madness: it's a neurotic's safety-valve, or an attention-drawing symptom of a death-wish. Such an interpretation is not anachronistic, for studies of melancholia were available to Shakespeare (Timothy Bright's *Treatise of Melancholy*, 1586, is deemed by scholars to be another of the sources); and, even without the use of such treatises, Shakespeare's knowledge of himself and his contemporaries could have provided plenty of information about neurotic psychology: the ill-fated Earl of Essex, friend of Shakespeare's patron the Earl of Southampton, has been cited as a model for Hamlet's temperament. Another type of scansion would justify the feigned madness not on grounds of strategic or psychological plausibility but rather on grounds of its dramatic value: Hamlet in his 'deranged' guise can adopt partly the role of court jester, partly the role of wise fool, partly that of the satiric spokesman on corruption; and his aberrant guise fruitfully generates dramatic suspense—will Claudius and his agents penetrate the fool's mask worn by Hamlet? If so, and they realise the threat that Hamlet offers, what action will they take?

Hamlet, then, is a character who is being pushed into certain shapes and patterns of action by the pressure of source-traditions; he is being pulled into other shapes by Shakespeare's sense of stagecraft and theatrical interest; he is being stretched and moulded by Shakespeare's personal preoccupations and observation of his times; and the result can be construed in ways which will vary remarkably with the interpreters' own prejudices or principles. Comparison with the available sources, coupled with our knowledge of Shakespeare's development prior to *Hamlet*, gives us a stronger sense of what, even allowing for our large ignorance of the lost *Ur-Hamlet*, are likely to be the most distinctive Shakespearian developments of the Amleth–Hamlet tradition. First, the greater realism of treatment of character and event, the action taking place in a plausibly contemporaneous setting; second, the far greater range and intelligence of philosophical discussion; third, the compression and intensification of the action—which includes an immense multiplication of ironies, related to the marked increase in internal analogues, parallels, contrasts and comparisons; and fourth, a sustained brilliance of eloquence and an intensely sensuous linguistic self-awareness. The action is being constantly 'universalised': which means that the richly metaphoric working of the material, constantly linking the particular to the general, tends to relate the action to a far wider range of common experience and familiar problems than could ever—or (to make a probably over-generous concession) could any longer—have been the case with the ancient saga of Amleth.

And what of the famous 'delay'? In Saxo and Belleforest the hero delays considerably longer than Shakespeare's Hamlet: the ancient hero took far more than a year (apparently several years) before slaying the usurper; whereas our Hamlet completes his task within a few months. What matters is that in Saxo and Belleforest the hero never gives any impression of delay. It's not only that he is so busy, it's also the case that since he retains partly-supernatural powers of divination and foresight, we are encouraged to believe that his every action, however seemingly eccentric and pointless, furthers his revenge; he even prepares the circumstances of the eventual holocaust at the palace before embarking for England, and in the massacre he uses those barbed rods he'd prepared so long ago. Our Hamlet, by contrast, moves in a far less magical and shamanistic world; it's civilised, Christianised, and subject to the credible vagaries of modern existence; humans have grown internally, in introspective capacity; and (perhaps following Hieronymo's example) he can problematise as a blameworthy delay what in Saxo could seem a matter of devious but deliberate progress. Some features of *Hamlet* encourage us to postulate comprehensive solutions to the problem; other features will make us doubt those solutions. *Hamlet* is a text which exposes the nature of the problematic in literature. It sensitively registers ideological contradictions (e.g. within and between Christianity, concepts of honour, Elizabethan political orthodoxy, and burgeoning empiricism) which, lacking full resolution within the play, partly account for the disorder subsequently displayed by interpreters.

The next stage in our discussion will be a consideration of some features of *Hamlet* which jeer at lovers of comprehensive, unitary explanations, and which may disconcert any readers who still think of this play as 'an organic whole'.

THE UNCERTAIN DATE

Shakespeare's *Hamlet* was registered in 1602 and first published in 1603; but the evidence to establish its dates of writing and first performance is lax, and suffices only for want of better. Francis Meres's *Palladis Tamia* (registered in 1598) gives a list of Shakespeare's works; and two of the plays which Meres does not mention are *Julius Caesar* and *Hamlet*, so scholars are led to assume that neither appeared until after 1598. *Julius Caesar* was performed in October 1599, and *Hamlet* is believed to have followed it—a belief encouraged by Horatio's speech at I.i. 116–23, which brings details of the Roman play to mind. Gabriel Harvey, in the marginal note we have quoted previously, observed: 'The younger sort takes much delight in Shakespeares Venus, & Adonis; but his Lucrece, & his tragedie of Hamlet, Prince of Denmarke, haue it in them, to please the wiser sort.'[9] This note apparently predates the arrest and execution of the Earl of Essex in February 1601. So, taken together, these bits of evidence make it seem feasible that *Hamlet* was first performed in 1600, give or take a couple of months. One snag is that *Hamlet*, II.ii. 336–58, refers to a theatrical controversy (about the challenge offered by the juvenile actors at the Blackfriars Theatre) which reached its peak in the middle of 1601. Professor Harold Jenkins concludes that though the play was performed by February, the passage about the juvenile actors was added 'about or soon after the middle of 1601'.[10]

Such matters of dating are obviously important, given that the comprehension and evaluation of a text naturally depend on assumptions about its date. If *Hamlet*, as we know it, had actually been written in 1595, it would seem even better—precociously brilliant. Another important matter is the implication of the scholarly belief that Shakespeare revised his *Hamlet* so as to incorporate that topical allusion to the boy actors. The implication is that when Shakespeare had written a play, it was not fixed and sacrosanct; he could return to it, adding bits here and perhaps cutting bits there, tinkering, reshaping; responding to contemporary pressures and controversies, expanding, censoring, rethinking; a fictional Denmark could even, for a while, be blended with familiar England. And other people (fellow-actors, prompt-men, scriveners, printers) were also influencing and sometimes rewriting the text. Shakespeare's plays were more mobile, pliable and protean than we initially assume.

Scholars generally regard the Second Quarto as the most authoritative of the early texts of *Hamlet*. Yet the Second Quarto lacks that discussion of the juvenile players which complicates the dating and which, demonstrably, has considerable thematic force within the play. Even those editors who emphasise the merits of the Second Quarto usually fill the gap by using the Folio version there. Thus we are reminded that editorial work is a creative and evaluative activity; even a subtly reticent and oblique mode of autobiography.

In this book I follow the example of many other critics in adopting the convenient assumption that Shakespeare's *Hamlet* first appeared in 1600. It's a reasonable assumption, given the available evidence. But that evidence does not exclude the possibility of an earlier date (particularly when we recall that Meres's list omits some early plays); so one of the foundations of critical judgement is insecure. Shakespeare may, in the 1590s, have produced a tentative script to be subsequently modified.

THE ABSENCE OF AN AUTHORITATIVE TEXT

Hamlet is an editor's nightmare. There are three substantive early texts: the First Quarto (Q1, 1603), the Second Quarto (Q2, 1604-5) and the First Folio (F, 1623). Q2 is better than the others but is still very faulty, so a common practice of

modern editors is to construct a text of *Hamlet* which takes
chunks from Q2 and bits from Q1 and F; the editors then
modernise in varying degrees the spelling, punctuation and
stage-directions (adding new stage-directions), and where
the text seems obscure or garbled they endeavour to emend
and clarify it.

The First Quarto is a 'memorially reconstructed' version:
apparently the actor who played both Marcellus and
Lucianus wrote down (or dictated) what he recalled of the
play, and the printers used the resultant script. The evidence
for this view is that whereas the speeches of Marcellus and
Lucianus seem intact, those of the other characters often
seem reduced or garbled. The outcome is a short play, 2,154
lines in length. Nevertheless, Q1 contains passages not
found in other texts; notably a speech in which Gertrude
agrees to conceal and assist any stratagem of Hamlet's
against the king, and a related scene in which Horatio
reports to Gertrude the failure of Claudius' scheme to have
Hamlet killed in England. A recent editor suggests that
'these speeches of the Queen peculiar to Q1 appear to derive
from the reporter's own attempt to sustain a coherent plot
when memory faltered'.[11] The presumed corruption of Q1
notwithstanding, it is commonly accepted as a guide not
only in the case of some stage-directions but also in the case
of various textual readings.

The Second Quarto, on the other hand, is very long; at
3,723 lines, the longest of Shakespeare's plays—almost
twice as long as *Macbeth*. It is supposed to have been printed
from 'foul papers': i.e., from an untidy manuscript by
Shakespeare. Some of the very details which indicate an
authentically Shakespearian script are those which tend not
to survive in modern editions. For example, the stage-
direction at the beginning of the Polonius–Reynaldo scene is
'*Enter old Polonius, with his man or two*'. Since the only
requisite parts in this scene are those of Polonius and
Reynaldo, modern editors usually change the stage-
direction accordingly: for example, to '*Enter old Polonius,*

with his man Reynaldo'. The critical significance of the original, rather tentative direction is considerable. It suggests that when Shakespeare began to write this scene he had not clearly envisaged how many actors or speaking-parts would be needed: Shakespeare worked by a mixture of planning and improvisation, some matters being clear in advance, others being unclear. We may also note that when editors have to choose between words which seem to be authentically Shakespearian and words which (for practical purposes) seem more precise, they are quite capable of choosing the latter rather than the former.

Q2 contains many small textual corruptions, where the compositors had difficulty in reading Shakespeare's handwriting or were simply careless; and sometimes they printed words or phrases which Shakespeare had intended to delete, these being 'first thoughts' subsequently revised— but both the first and second versions have been set in type by the compositors. The manuscript may not have come in an unrevised form: it may well have been emended by a playhouse book-keeper before reaching the printing-shop. The printers then made attempts to improve the manuscript, by regularising grammar and metre and by imposing their own conventions of punctuation. Furthermore, they consulted a copy of Q1 (particularly while working on Act I), so that the 'foul' Q2 has been contaminated by readings of the 'bad' Q1. And while the sheets of Q2 were being printed, a 'corrector' made small changes—some of which were fresh errors. Finally, although Q2 is long, it still omits two very interesting passages, one describing Denmark as a prison (II.ii. 239–69), the other dealing with the popularity of the boy actors (II.ii. 335–58). The reason for these omissions may be censorship: King James's wife was Anne of Denmark, and by 1604 the boy actors had become accredited as 'The Children of the Queen's Revels'; but any such censorship to avert royal displeasure was inconsistent, given that the passage which describes Danes as notorious drunkards (I.iv. 17–38) was allowed to remain in Q2 while being absent from Q1 and F.

It might be expected that the First Folio of 1623 would provide the best version of *Hamlet*, since that Folio volume was prepared by two of Shakespeare's fellow-actors, Heminge and Condell, ostensibly as a memorial tribute to their colleague who had died in 1616. Certainly F contains over seventy lines not found in Q2, and its stage-directions (e.g. '*In scuffling they change Rapiers*') provide useful clarifications of the actions. The snags, however, are these. First, F lacks 230 lines that were present in Q2; second, F is based partly on Q2, and is contaminated by some of Q2's corruptions; third, some of the small additions in F are believed to be actors' interpolations; and fourth, F has a variety of new corruptions, many deriving from its team of compositors and particularly from the hapless compositor known to posterity only as 'B'.

Thus, any scholar hired to produce a new edition of *Hamlet* would encounter excruciating difficulties. Q1 is closest, chronologically, to the time at which *Hamlet* was first conceived and acted, but is woefully short and extensively garbled. Q2 is almost embarrassingly long (few stage-productions offer so full a version), yet is still incomplete and tainted by corruptions. F is also incomplete and tainted. Each one has significant passages which the other two lack. A new editor might well have to draw on all three, and the resultant text would contain material not only by Shakespeare but also by various copyists, compositors, correctors, actors and previous editors. Another scholar, faced with the same task, would produce a different text— probably very similar in the main, but certainly different in detail; and some of those details could conceivably be quite crucial to a given critical interpretation. Through all changes, an identity remains; *Hamlet* isn't going to emerge as a comedy or a cookery-book; but the critics will repeatedly be interpreting data which have already been manipulated, tidied, rearranged and rephrased in the light of the editor's critical assumptions.

In Shakespeare's lifetime, the text of *Hamlet* was being adapted, expanded, cut; and, when it was performed, more changes were being made: actors might leave out some speeches to save time and expense, or they might embellish their roles with an ad-lib here or there, an expressive groan or exclamation, a helpful cue, an explanatory phrase. If Shakespeare could look over our shoulders at a modern scholarly edition of *Hamlet*, much of it would look strange and foreign to him: the modernisations of spelling and punctuation would give the text a quaintly exotic quality, and he would probably wince at numerous corruptions and garblings. He might tell us that his preferred version had evidently not survived in print, so that editors have been permutating scripts he would regard as inferior; or he might complain that the modern scholarly edition strives to fix and ossify what he'd intended to leave relatively loose and pliable. He might say: 'Look, we performed this play in various ways at the Globe, in a different way at Court, and when we went on tour we made more changes. Why does Hamlet delay, you ask? If I'd known, I would have said so in the play. Hold your peace, or next you'll be asking me what Iago's real motive was!'

"TIS HERE, BUT YET CONFUS'D': EVIDENCE OF CONFUSION IN PLOT AND CHARACTERISATION

Soon after *Hamlet* was staged, Shakespeare created one of his most paradoxically engaging villains: Iago. What makes Iago 'paradoxically engaging' is that although he remains cynically destructive, he stands in a closer conceptual relationship to the audience than do any of the virtuous characters: through his asides and soliloquies he seems to take us into his confidence as if we were his accomplices. He fleetingly resembles a contrasting mirror-image of Hamlet:

Hamlet has a strong motive for revenge, but is preoccupied by delay; Iago is preoccupied by revenge, and pauses to seek adequate motives for it. Uncannily, Iago resembles an artist, a rapid author who progresses by a mixture of planning and improvisation while we eavesdrop on the process. As Iago works on the human materials around him, bending them to a general purpose while being uncertain of the details of his plan, so, we may imagine, Shakespeare the dramatist worked on his inherited source-materials, being clear about some broad lines of adaptation but less certain of details of plot and characterisation. Like Iago, Shakespeare may often have reflected: ''Tis here, but yet confus'd.' The following sections offer evidence of his uncertainty and suggest that *Hamlet*, as we know it, remains a record of 'work in progress'.

Horatio: Resident or Visitor?

Horatio is undoubtedly a Dane, and in Act I, scene i, he is a recognised authority on Danish matters: he knew the late king well and is familiar with current political realities and rumours in Denmark. Yet, in the next scene, he is a visitor from Wittenberg who has come for the royal funeral; while, in Act I, scene iv, he is ignorant of an internationally-notorious Danish custom (excessive social drinking) which Hamlet, 'native here', has to explain to him. (Even within Act I, scene ii, there is apparent inconsistency, for Horatio says 'I knew your father' in a context which implies that Horatio knew him well, but also says 'I saw him once' in a way which implies that Horatio saw the late king on only one occasion.) Certainly Horatio has been abroad as a student at Wittenberg (like Hamlet), but that does not explain how he manages to be both familiar and unfamiliar with Danish matters extending over a long period. There is, of course, a functional explanation of the inconsistency: an obvious dramatic pretext for imparting useful information to the audience is to let one character in a particular scene have the role of enlightener of a person who is (or persons who are) in a state of relative ignorance. In Act I, scene i, Horatio is the informant and the watchmen are relatively ignorant; in Act I, scene iv, it is now Hamlet's turn to be the informant, while Horatio slips into the role of an enquiring visitor; and again, in V.ii. 82–9, Horatio's unfamiliarity with the court is the cue for Hamlet's caustic epitome of Osric. (The characterisation of Osric, too, is inconsistent: Hamlet introduces him as a landowning 'chuff', a boorish countryman with more money than sense; yet the Osric whom we meet sounds far more like a well-educated but needy courtier who, to improve his prospects, obsequiously strives to ingratiate himself with his employers.) Our understanding of the fictional Denmark is thus furthered at the cost of slippage in Horatio's characterisation; and this has a bearing on the engima of Hamlet's character. In the presentation of Hamlet, too, there may be some slippage as circumstances change: he may be a palimpsestic creation, layered and mosaiced, as a result not only of friction between the sources and Shakespeare's interests but also of the varying imaginative opportunities that a pliable assemblage permits Shakespeare to realise.

Fortinbras: Rebellious Hot-Head or Worthy Heir?

Horatio is undoubtedly an honest man of reliable judgement; and in the opening scene he describes 'young Fortinbras' as a person 'Of unimprovèd mettle, hot and full' (raw, immature, impetuous) who has 'Shark'd up a list of lawless resolutes' (hastily and indiscriminately gathered a gang of desperadoes) for the invasion of Denmark. Yet, in Act IV, scene iv, the same Fortinbras speaks like a mature diplomat when he seeks renewed permission from Claudius for the march across Denmark to Poland, and his 'lawless resolutes' are now a disciplined army—all the more disciplined, given that they are going to battle for a worthless patch of ground. Eventually, the dying Hamlet prophesies the election of Fortinbras to the throne of Denmark, and the candidate promptly arrives (having completed his Polish campaign) to assert that he has an old claim to the throne and to organise Hamlet's funeral rites. The character of Fortinbras seems to have changed to suit dramatic convenience. At the play's opening, suspense is generated by the news that Denmark is threatened by a gang of adventurers; while, at the play's end, Fortinbras has become a highly convenient *deus ex machina*, having acquired appropriate stature to superintend the concluding ceremonies and to fill the vacant throne. We may speculate that if Shakespeare had had the leisure to revise the play, he would have toned down the early emphasis on Fortinbras' immaturity and the lawlessness of his followers, would have provided an early indication that Fortinbras had a valid claim to the Danish throne, and would have offered some hints (before the theatrically coincidental arrival in Act V) that Fortinbras, having completed the Polish expedition, intended a visit to the Danish court. Part of the apparent inconsistency in the presentation of his character can be explained if we assume that the interview with his angry uncle (reported in II.ii. 65–71) led to a rapid chastening and maturing of his character, and this in turn adds to the dramatic structure of ironic analogies, given that Hamlet vehemently declined to be chastened by the warnings (in I.ii. 92–107) from his own uncle. By such speculations and assumptions, however, we walk into the familiar ambush of *Hamlet*: provoked by its reticences and corrugations, we seek, as so many have done, to rewrite, smooth and rationalise the text. It is quite possible that the playwright, when initially depicting Fortinbras as unruly, had not foreseen his eventual role as restorer of order. Lucio in *Measure for Measure* shows that Shakespeare is quite capable of using one nominal character to perform the functions of two characters.

The Proleptic Planning of The Murder of Gonzago

In II.ii. 531–6, Hamlet asks the first player to arrange a performance, the following night, of *The Murder of Gonzago*; the player agrees both to do so and to include in this play 'some dozen or sixteen lines' specially written by Hamlet. Yet, later in the scene (from line 543), the solitary Hamlet reproaches himself for inactivity, and continues:

> About, my brains. Hum—I have heard
> That guilty creatures sitting at a play
> Have, by the very cunning of the scene,
> Been struck so to the soul that presently
> They have proclaim'd their malefactions.
> For murder, though it have no tongue, will speak
> With most miraculous organ. I'll have these players
> Play something like the murder of my father
> Before mine uncle. I'll observe his looks . . . . .

Shakespeare seems to have got things back to front. The instructions to the first player show that Hamlet has already planned to prick Claudius' conscience by means of the murder-play, and, furthermore, has already decided to add new material to the old text so as to make it even more appropriate to Claudius' situation. Nevertheless, fifty lines later we see Hamlet casting around for a stratagem and alighting on the notion of a play that will make Claudius blench. The sad consequence is that Hamlet appears to suffer an authorially-inflicted bout of amnesia. The author might reply, however: 'No: it's *editorially*-inflicted; intelligent players and directors have the sense to cut the text; indeed, I made this play unusually long so that they would have greater freedom to trim and rearrange its components'.

Hamlet: Thirty-Year-Old Adolescent?

In Act V, scene i, the grave-digger makes doubly clear that Hamlet must be thirty years old. He says that he himself has been at work 'since that very day that young Hamlet was born': 'I have been sexton here, man and boy, thirty years.' This is confirmed by the subsequent information about Yorick. When Hamlet was a child, Yorick used to play with him, and Yorick has now been in the grave 'three and twenty years', which tallies quite reasonably with the claim that Hamlet is thirty. The grave-digger, whose memory seems disconcertingly acute, also states that it is thirty years since Hamlet's father slew old Fortinbras; so young Fortinbras is, at the youngest, over twenty-nine and a few months, and Horatio, who (in I.i.) seemed to have personal recollection of the slaying of old Fortinbras, could therefore be as old as forty, even though he is Hamlet's fellow-student at Wittenberg.

Elsewhere, the impression given by much of the text is that Fortinbras is about twenty, Hamlet no older, and Horatio perhaps two or three years older than Hamlet—possibly twenty-one or twenty-two. The account of Fortinbras in Act I, scene i, as we have noted, gives a clear impression of a headstrong, rash, impetuous young man, as yet immature and in need of reprimands from his prudent uncle. The sense that Horatio is about twenty-one or twenty-two derives from our knowledge that though he is young enough to be a student, he behaves soberly and judiciously, and is respected by Hamlet for his stoical composure. Generally, Hamlet himself seems to be about eighteen or nineteen. His oscillations in mood, his bursts of energy, his enthusiasms and introspections, his passionately prurient disgust at his mother's remarriage—all these contribute to a sense that the prince has not totally emerged from adolescence. Laertes and Polonius, in their warnings to Ophelia in Act I, scene iii, emphasise his unreliable youthfulness.

So the grave-digger's information that Hamlet is thirty seems starkly anomalous; it threatens to disrupt our general conception of the relationships between the major characters and, particularly, of the important thematic contrast that the play has established between age and youth, maturity and immaturity.

Professor Harold Jenkins' explanation is that Shakespeare's purpose in this part of the graveyard scene was not to give us precise information about Hamlet's age but rather to let the grave-digger be sufficiently old to act as a kind of thematic chorus. His career spans, and draws together, crucial events of the plot.

> As Hamlet's talk with the grave-digger thus links the grave-digger's occupation with the term of Hamlet's life, will it not seem to us that the hero has come face to face with his own destiny? The companion of his carefree childhood has already been a generation underground. Must not he himself, however 'young' or old, be ready for what will come?[12]

The obvious difficulty with this theory is that the grave-digger could perfectly well have performed such a thematic retrospective function without specifying a seemingly anomalous age for Hamlet; he could have recalled the fight with old Fortinbras and the death of Yorick, and generally chatted about time, change and mortality, without being so numerically specific. It seems over-optimistic for a commentator to suggest, as Jenkins does, that we should remember the 'thirty years' in relationship only to the grave-digger and not in relationship to Hamlet; we expect any dramatist who is in his right senses to be able to provide information about one character without thereby inducing inconsistency with the data concerning another character. If the text tallies with what Shakespeare actually wrote, the most likely explanation of the anomaly would seem to be that while establishing the grave-digger's character,

Shakespeare committed a mathematical blunder which subsequent revision—had revision ever taken place and been published—could have erased. (We know that in other plays, notably *Measure for Measure*, *Othello* and *The Winter's Tale*, his chronological specificity led to inconsistency; and it's relevant that the mathematics of Claudius' wager, at V.ii. 162–4, appear self-contradictory.) As it stands, the text here seems irredeemably erratic. We seek a solution, and we encounter an opacity; but we learn a useful general lesson about the 'dynamics of the problematic' in a literary text.

What makes a textual opacity conspicuous is (1) that it has a bright fringe, a question-begging circumference; (2) that the reader is committed to maximising the unity and intelligibility of the text as a whole; and (3) that elsewhere the text rewards such commitment on the reader's part. The sense of frustration induced by one part of the text is thus proportionate to the sense of gratification granted by other parts.

The Strange Case of Invisible Incest

Even before his encounter with the ghost, Hamlet is appalled by the nature of his mother's marriage to Claudius: 'O most wicked speed! To post/ With such dexterity to incestuous sheets!' The ghost, in turn, is vehement in his condemnation of the incest: Claudius is 'that incestuous, that adulterate beast':

> Let not the royal bed of Denmark be
> A couch for luxury and damned incest.

In marrying Claudius, Gertrude was marrying her brother-in-law; and, according to the canonical law of both the Roman Catholic and the Anglican Churches (influenced by Leviticus 20:21), such a marriage was indeed incestuous and prohibited. (Not until the Marriage Enabling Act of 1960 did it become lawful in England.)

A peculiar anomaly in the play is, therefore, that while Hamlet and the ghost are well aware of this scandalous event, and though the remarriage of Gertrude was fully and ceremonially public, nobody in the court seems to have noticed any incest at all. Furthermore, the text vigorously precludes any assumption that this obliviousness is a sympton of a morally decadent or myopic court: one function of the exchanges between Laertes, Polonius and Ophelia in Act I, scene iii, and between Polonius and Reynaldo in Act II, scene i, is to emphasise that this court is concerned to maintain traditional moral proprieties in sexual conduct.

One way of dealing with this problem presents itself. As we are reminded by the explanation of Ophelia's burial in sanctified ground (V.i. 219–27), English audiences knew that there was one law for the rich and another for the poor: more precisely, that monarchs held the power to circumvent canonical law. The most famous example was the marriage of Henry VIII to Catherine of Aragon. Catherine was the widow of Henry's brother Arthur; but Henry was able to marry her because, by diplomacy with Rome, he had secured a papal dispensation. Early audiences might therefore have assumed that a similar situation prevailed in the world of *Hamlet*. The courtiers of Elsinore, accepting that a papal dispensation had waived the traditional prohibition, could see the marriage of Claudius and Gertrude as lawful and proper; but Hamlet and the ghost, having personal reason to resent bitterly the remarriage of Gertrude, are concerned with the spirit rather than the letter of the law, and see a reality of incest which, in their eyes, has not been dispelled by any ecclesiastical parchment.

What makes this way of dealing with the problem so wilful and wishful is that it provides a clarification that the play defiantly declines to provide. The resultant lacuna increases the variability in the critics' interpretations of Hamlet himself. More information about the legal and ecclesiastical circumstances of the remarriage would have provided guidance; without it, an important element in Hamlet's attitude lacks a precise criterion and definition. By accident or design, the play thus exhibits an ideological disarray; a conflict within and between religious, political and dramatic conceptions of sexual order and transgression.

An Illogical and Humiliated Ghost?

The dominant critical opinion is that the ghost is who he says he is; a minority opinion[13] is that he is the devil (or a devil) in disguise. In fact the mystery of the ghost's provenance is vigorously established at the outset of the play and then, as the action proceeds, is not so much solved as dispelled, and not so much dispelled as merely outdistanced and superseded by other and more engrossing matters.

When the ghost appears to Hamlet, the possibility that it may be diabolic is clearly expressed by both Hamlet and Horatio. On hearing the apparition's story, however, Hamlet appears to be convinced by it; and subsequently he tells Horatio that 'It is an honest ghost'. But his suspicions return, and the purpose of staging *The Murder of Gonzago* is to test simultaneously Claudius and the apparition. Claudius evinces guilt, and the prince, elated, says, 'I'll take the ghost's word for a thousand pound'. A safe bet, however, is not the same as sound knowledge; and even a veracious ghost could still be diabolic, since the devil can tell the truth to suit his purposes. Nevertheless, most members of the audience are likely to assume that the ghost's provenance has now been established and to concentrate on other matters. The apparition returns when Hamlet is berating his mother; spectators who believe that it is 'honest' will note that its uxorious concern for Gertrude tallies with what it said in I.v. 84–8 and with the sense that this spirit is still 'human, all too human' in its character.

The 'diabolonian' interpreters notice rightly that this ghost not only 'stalks away' when Horatio invokes heaven but also retreats guiltily when the cock (associated with Christ) crows—suspicious conduct indeed; that the apparition urges a bloody course upon a prince made suggestible by melancholy; and that at its final appearance, its concern is not merely to protect Gertrude but mainly to whet Hamlet's 'almost blunted purpose'. To many Roman Catholics, it was a reasonable supposition that if ghosts existed, they were the wandering souls of sufferers in purgatory; but, at the Reformation, Protestants had declared the abolition of purgatory: so the predominant Protestant explanation of ghosts was that they were devils in disguise, busily spreading evil. On the other hand, we may note that Shakespeare's other plays maintain the usual convention that ghosts are who they purport to be; that this particular ghost sounds convincing (its tones are not satanic or ironic but sound plausibly like those of a doubly-betrayed—if self-righteous—warrior-king); that the allegation of Claudius' guilt is fully confirmed by the malefactor; and that when Hamlet does fulfil the ghost's behest by slaying Claudius, the action is condoned by Horatio and can even be regarded as fulfilment of the will of divine providence.

If, however, we accept this orthodox view that the apparition is indeed the spirit of King Hamlet, we find that the ghost is morally and theologically contradictory. He confirms the existence of purgatory and, thereby, of heaven, hell and the Christian God; yet he commands Hamlet to carry out an anti-Christian task: bloody revenge. 'Thou shalt not kill'; 'Vengeance is mine; I shall repay', had declared the God of both the Old Testament and the New;[14] and Elizabethan spokesmen had often emphasised that God forbids revenge. Clarence in *Richard III* (I.iv. 212–16) sums up the orthodox claim:

If God will be revengèd for the deed,
O, know you yet He doth it publicly.
Take not the quarrel from His pow'rful arm;
He needs no indirect or lawless course
To cut off those that have offended Him.

One complication is that, as Belleforest pointed out when
recounting the story of 'Hamblet', biblical warrant could be
found for private vengeance; another is that Elizabethan
politicians (notably in the 'Bond of Association', 1584)
advocated 'uttermost revenge' against would-be usurpers of
the throne. So the theatrical convention that the fulfilled
avenger must himself perish was sometimes breached—
usually when, as in the case of Malcolm's 'great revenge'
against Macbeth, the victim's crimes had been particularly
heinous and the avenger could be seen as the saviour of
traditional moral and political order.

What, in *Hamlet*, tends to make the ghost's injunction of
revenge seem morally and theologically questionable is the
moral and theological sophistication of the context. A
Hamlet who can recall that 'the Everlasting' has 'fix'd his
canon 'gainst self-slaughter' is fully capable of recalling that
the Everlasting has also fixed his canon 'gainst revenge and
murder. There is a soliloquy which the prince never utters
but which is easily · within his range of character and
reflection; it goes roughly like this:

'Thou shalt not kill', th'Almighty's words declare;
'Hamlet, revenge', enjoins my father's voice,
An embassage from death. Each way I'm snar'd.
O limèd soul, that struggling to be free
Art more engag'd! If God will Claudius slay,
Why, God may do't, without my stir; for me,
Though with such high wrongs I am struck to
      th'quick,
Yet with my nobler reason 'gainst my fury

Do I take part: the rarer action is
In virtue than in vengeance.

This pastiche borrows some words from Claudius, to
suggest that Claudius' plight is not totally different from
Hamlet's (for both men register the sense of being ensnared);
a few words from Macbeth; and some famous lines from
Prospero, as a reminder that Shakespeare's plays frequently
and tellingly commend mercy rather than revenge. Hamlet
cannot utter such a soliloquy, for that would make the very
premises of the plot appear self-contradictory. But
reflections of this kind are evoked in us by some of Hamlet's
suspicions of the ghost as well as by his procrastinations;
and we see that the eventual death of Claudius occurs not as
a result of any Machiavellian murder-plot by the prince but
very soon after Hamlet has shrugged off Horatio's warnings
about the impending duel by making a strongly fatalistic
utterance: 'If it be now, 'tis not to come; if it be not to come,
it will be now; if it be not now, yet it will come.' In the
theatre, one of the functions of *The Murder of Gonzago* may
be to persuade the audience that the problem of the ghost is
solved if the ghost is proved to be truthful, when actually the
members of the audience have thereby been deflected from
focusing their misgivings on the far greater problem—the
theological anomaly of a divinely-sanctioned injunction to
revenge.

If the ghost initially seems anomalous, of ambiguous
provenance, and in various ways anachronistic (a warrior-
king accosting a civilised world, a spectre imposing a
Senecan demand on a sophisticated court), we may be
gratified by that sequence in which Hamlet seems to effect an
appropriately conceptual retaliation. In Act I, scene v, after
the apparition has withdrawn, Hamlet urges his
companions to swear secrecy:

Hamlet.   Never make known what you have seen
                       tonight . . . . .

	Nay, but swear't . . . . .
	Upon my sword.
Marcellus.	We have sworn, my lord, already.
Hamlet.	Indeed, upon my sword, indeed.
Ghost.	(Cries under the stage) Swear.
Hamlet.	Ah ha, boy, say'st thou so? Art thou there, truepenny?
	Come on, you hear this fellow in the cellarage.
	Consent to swear.
Horatio.	Propose the oath, my lord.
Hamlet.	Never to speak of this that you have seen.
	Swear by my sword.
Ghost.	Swear. [They swear.]
Hamlet.	Hic et ubique? Then we'll shift our ground.
	Come hither, gentlemen,
	And lay your hands again upon my sword.
	Swear by my sword
	Never to speak of this that you have heard.
Ghost.	Swear by his sword. [They swear.]
Hamlet.	Well said, old mole. Canst work i'th' earth so fast?
	A worthy pioner! Once more remove, good friends.

This is one of the oddest and (for directors) most tricky
sequences in the play. In a tense and crucial scene, farce and
conceptual breakdown suddenly impend. Embarrassingly,
there's the ghost again, speaking from below ground,
parroting Hamlet's words and (apparently needlessly) also
urging the men to swear; furthermore Hamlet, as though
seeing that the situation has incongruous resemblances to
farce, enters the new spirit of the game by addressing the
ghost jauntily as 'boy', 'truepenny', 'this fellow in the
cellarage', as an 'old mole' and a sapper ('worthy pioner').
While the men move from one part of the battlements to
another, the ghost moves beneath, tracking their course; so

the phrase 'old mole' is disturbingly apt mockery. Particularly, it's the reference to 'this fellow in the cellarage' that accentuates the oddity, for momentarily the flagstones of the high battlements of Elsinore dissolve into the planks of the apron stage at the Globe Theatre—planks beneath which an actor crouches in the dusty gloom. Furthermore, as if to precipitate the sense of the ghost's anachronism and ambivalent provenance, Hamlet's words invoke the devices of an out-of-date form of drama, the Morality play in which a Vice might jest with a supposedly subterranean demon.[15]

A critic who was also an amateur psychologist could, of course, endeavour to salvage the situation as realism. He could say: 'It's a familiar fact that a person who is undergoing considerable stress or tension may seek psychological relief in jesting or buffoonery: we've all felt the impulse to giggle or snigger during some solemn or frightening incident. Hamlet is neurotic, anyway; and after the extreme tension of the face-to-face encounter with the ghost, his relief that he has survived the ordeal now finds expression in a flurry of mockingly patronising references to the apparition. This is realism of a high order.' To which one answer is, 'That is not how it seems in the theatre. There, it seems odd.' We in the audience have been taking things seriously, and suddenly a prominent character seems to mock our earnestness by a jesting which jars us into a recognition of fictional conventions. The theatrical illusion is briefly eroded as, with 'conceptual bad taste', Hamlet exercises an unconventional freedom within it, evoking devices that our imagination has striven to conceal.

Whether the ghost, for a moment, is transformed into the actor scuttling about in the 'cellarage' under the stage, or is merely shown to be comically analogous to that scuttling actor, his dignity is humbled; and the drama has here exercised more play (levity, sportiveness, flexibility), than we can comfortably accommodate. Here, as elsewhere, *Hamlet* is a freer and more volatile work than the tragedy we are usually told about.

Implicitly, there is a further humiliation for the ghost when Hamlet utters the 'To be or not to be' soliloquy (III.i. 56–88). Hamlet speaks of death as

The undiscover'd country, from whose bourn
No traveller returns

—as if he has forgotten the recent return of a traveller in spectral armour; and he speaks also of death as a sleep in which we may have bad dreams, as if he has forgotten the ghost's specification of purgatory. A severe comment might be that Shakespeare, while eloquently expressing a modern uncertainty about death and the afterlife, has fallen into blatant inconsistency with the theological premises of the plot. A kinder comment might be that Hamlet is being consistently inconsistent: just as, in Act I, he had veered between bold action and melancholy introspection, so here he offers a predictably unpredictable meditation. In his previous soliloquy he had reproached himself for tardiness in proceeding to revenge; now he reflects that reflection deters one from suicidal resolve. If we say, 'He is suicidally melancholy because he is disillusioned with his mother', we supply a connective explanation that the new soliloquy signally lacks. Hence, in part, the fame of this meditation on 'To be or not to be': the soliloquy solicits the attentions of memorisers and anthology-editors, for it is so readily detachable, so seemingly self-contained and transferable. An opportunistic vagrancy in Shakespeare's imagination has been licensed by Hamlet; or, alternatively, Hamlet, by deeds and reflections that veer to the side of the predictable, exhibits a new and realistic freedom in characterisation; or, speculatively, Shakespeare provided a speech that could be delivered if the audience welcomed sophistication but could easily be cut if the audience wanted swifter action. The soliloquy lives on because it is true: it eloquently expresses what so many people have sometimes thought and felt; indeed, it helped to create a temperament of sensitive agnosticism whose homeland was the Victorian rather than the Elizabethan age; and it is true as an epitomising enactment of the very process of exploratory introspection.

Critics who seek a Christian affirmation in *Hamlet* may emphasise the prince's eventual invocation of divine providence: 'We defy augury. There is special providence in the fall of a sparrow'.[16] Such trust in providence, however, seems to be mocked by the murder of Hamlet's father, by the ghost's commandment of revenge, and by the ghost's anxiety to 'whet' the 'almost blunted purpose'. One technical explanation of such inconsistency is that Shakespeare is deploying any theological notion which will serve to lubricate the impending movements of the plot; but the 'To be or not to be' soliloquy appears to retard rather than lubricate its progress, and thus illustrates the rule that a sense of realism is generated by ostensibly non-functional material. The more one seeks to make the play theologically consistent, the more one will sense, instead, not only a contradiction between the Christian emphasis on mercy and the vengeful ethic of 'honour' but also various contradictions within Christianity: for example, between its commendation of forgiveness and its praise of a punitive God, or between its exhortation to 'turn the other cheek' and its advocacy of militant action against sinners. By his reflections on 'the sleep of death' and its 'undiscover'd country', Hamlet—in defiance of the premises and closure of the play—voices a new agnosticism, the paradox of ephemeral man who seeks to explore in thought the dark encompassing eternities. *Hamlet* is the veering seismograph which registers the earth-tremors and landslides of ideology.

·2·
'Yet there be method in't':
The Co-ordination

In Chapter 1 I illustrated the case that might be offered by someone who wished to challenge the notion that the text of *Hamlet* is sufficiently reliable and co-ordinated to provide 'unifying' theories with a sound basis. In this chapter I go to the other extreme and illustrate the case that might be made by someone who wished to argue that *Hamlet* is a remarkably coherent and subtly-organised work.

THE INTERLINKED THEMES

If we look back over the plot, we see that its main structure is elegantly ironic: Claudius' crime leads to actions by Hamlet which provoke a sequence of reactions by Claudius, and these bring upon the usurper the destruction that he had planned for the prince. Certainly some material, as we have remarked, seems not to further the plot: notably the preparations for war (described in such detail in Act I, scene i) and the 'To be or not to be' soliloquy. But these two passages have ample thematic function: they are linked by the themes of 'action versus passivity', 'public and private warfare' and 'the value of life and the meaning of death'. Indeed, *Hamlet* offers a dense orchestration of interweaving and harmonising themes: the relationship between action and reflection; the ethics of revenge; the nature of honour; attitudes to death; 'appetite' as ambition, lust and intemperance; conflict between the older and the younger generations; fidelity and treachery; idealism and cynicism; actors, acting and action; 'mousetraps'; spies and spying; melancholia and madness; and man as both 'the beauty of the world' and 'this quintessence of dust'. Repeatedly the play looks over the edge of life into death, and though it offers contrasting vistas (unquiet slumbers, purgatory, flights of angels, politic worms, the transmutation of a Caesar into clay, or merely silence), the persistent questioning is a major co-ordinator. One could object, of course, that since thematic headings are usually spongy and flexible, a thematic scansion inevitably has the effect of linking what other modes of scansion might register as disparate; but the summary of the source-tales (in Chapter 1) has demonstrated that Shakespeare amplified the plot in ways which multiply ironic linkages and accentuate thematic continuities. For instance, Saxo and Belleforest portrayed only one vengeful son; Shakespeare portrays four.

THE VENGEFUL SONS

Fortinbras

In *Hamlet* we find not just one son seeking vengeance for a slain father, but four sons: Young Fortinbras, Hamlet, Laertes and Pyrrhus.

Fortinbras initially leads his so-called 'lawless resolutes' towards Denmark to regain lands lost by his father, who was slain by King Hamlet: so there is an ironic note of tardy recognition when, at the end of the play, the dying Hamlet ensures Fortinbras' succession to the Danish throne. Fortinbras obtains the redress which he had originally

sought, and more besides: he has not only regained his
father's lost lands but also acquired the whole kingdom of
Denmark. This consequence has potent thematic force:
Fortinbras, by abandoning his original vengeful quest, has
gained more than he could have envisaged; the campaign
against Poland, for a patch of land 'that hath in it no profit
but the name', has in the end proved vastly profitable,
because the return journey has brought Fortinbras to
Elsinore just in time to fill the power vacuum caused by the
destruction of the Hamlet dynasty; and he takes the throne
once occupied by a king who himself had assailed the
'Polacks'.[1] The story of Fortinbras thus seems to confirm
Hamlet's pious notion that

> There's a divinity that shapes our ends,
> Rough-hew them how we will.

Bloody intent, thwarted purpose, indirection, deflection
abroad, and eventual fulfilment of the original ambition:
these features of Fortinbras' story are also features of
Hamlet's. In Chapter 1 of this book we noted that one
alleged inconsistency in the account of Fortinbras is that
his 'lawless resolutes' turn into a well-disciplined army; but
it might readily be argued that Horatio's Danish patriotism
(or his credence of patriotic rumours) could explain his
pejorative account (I.i. 98–107) of Fortinbras' invaders.
Indeed, such an argument is well supported by the context:
Marcellus' description of the feverishly intensive war-
preparations in Denmark (strict watch-keeping, brazen
cannon being made, foreign markets scoured for weapons,
shipwrights working seven days a week, other workers on
night-shifts) makes clear that what is anticipated by the
Danes is a massive invasion by an army and no mere raid by
cut-throats. Subsequently, the speech by Fortinbras at the
start of Act IV, scene iv, though brief, is sufficient to
establish that he seems noble, princely, diplomatic and fit to
rule.

From the very first scene in which Hamlet appears, we are caught in a network of comparisons. Claudius' dealings there (from I.i. 17) concern firstly Fortinbras, who may be restrained by his uncle from his aggressive course; secondly, Laertes, who wishes to return to France and has his father's consent (thus a future vengeful son is introduced); and thirdly Hamlet, whose uncle fails to dissuade him from prolonging his mourning: so a theme of 'counselling by uncles' emerges. Later, in Act IV, scene iv, a further linkage is explicitly and systematically established between the careers of Fortinbras and Hamlet. On learning from the captain that the Norwegian army intends to fight the Poles for that 'little patch of ground / That hath in it no profit but the name', Hamlet scornfully observes:

Two thousand souls and twenty thousand ducats
Will not debate the question of this straw!

Then, when the others have gone, he begins the long and crucial meditation:

How all occasions do inform against me,
And spur my dull revenge. What is a man
If his chief good and market of his time
Be but to sleep and feed? A beast, no more.
Sure he that made us with such large discourse,
Looking before and after, gave us not
That capability and godlike reason
To fust in us unus'd. Now whether it be
Bestial oblivion, or some craven scruple
Of thinking too precisely on th'event—
A thought which, quarter'd, hath but one part wisdom
And ever three parts coward—I do not know
Why yet I live to say this thing's to do,
Sith I have cause, and will, and strength, and means
To do't. Examples gross as earth exhort me,
Witness this army of such mass and charge,

Led by a delicate and tender prince,
Whose spirit, with divine ambition puff'd,
Makes mouths at the invisible event,
Exposing what is mortal and unsure
To all that fortune, death, and danger dare,
Even for an eggshell. Rightly to be great
Is not to stir without great argument,
But greatly to find quarrel in a straw
When honour's at the stake. How stand I then,
That have a father kill'd, a mother stain'd,
Excitements of my reason and my blood,
And let all sleep, while to my shame I see
The imminent death of twenty thousand men
That, for a fantasy and trick of fame,
Go to their graves like beds, fight for a plot
Whereon the numbers cannot try the cause,
Which is not tomb enough and continent
To hide the slain? O, from this time forth,
My thoughts be bloody or be nothing worth.

The verse-movement is fluently flexible, supple and varied;
there is a high proportion of enjambed and mid-stopped
lines; the exposition of thought is generally lucid, moves
with seemingly natural logic from stage to stage, and well
creates the illusion that we are eavesdropping on someone
who is thinking aloud spontaneously. The gist of the
soliloquy is: 'I shouldn't waste time any longer; Fortinbras'
army goes resolutely into action in the name of honour, and
so should I.' Yet one irony is immediately apparent: in the
very act of saying this at such length, Hamlet is yet again
displaying that habit of protracted introspection which he
claims to be eschewing; indeed, there is irony within this
irony as he refers to

            some craven scruple
Of thinking too precisely on th'event—

> A thought which, quarter'd, hath but one part
>   wisdom
> And ever three parts coward

—for even here he is incorrigibly 'thinking too precisely' as he dissects such thinking into its ratio of wisdom to cowardice.

A larger irony is the extent to which the ostensible argument is undermined by its detail. In the very act of claiming that Fortinbras' army sets an example to be emulated, Hamlet describes that army's work in such a way as to suggest very good reasons why it should *not* be emulated. When he says that Fortinbras exposes

> what is mortal and unsure
> To all that fortune, death and danger dare,
> Even for an eggshell[,]

the last phrase, by its deliberate bathos, invites the audience to reflect that such action exhibits stupidity rather than courage. Again, the suggestion that the truly great 'find quarrel in a straw / When honour's at the stake' can invite the response, 'So much the worse for honour, then!' And if we recall the fates of Hotspur, Hector, Antony and Coriolanus, we see that there is good Shakespearian warrant for such sceptical misgivings. Repeatedly Hamlet's soliloquy emphasises the contradiction between 'honour' and common sense: the soldiers, 'for a fantasy and trick of fame', perish for a bit of land 'Which is not tomb enough and continent / To hide the slain'. So, although the argument leads Hamlet to conclude that he should henceforth be determinedly 'bloody', various details of his soliloquy have pointed towards a quite different conclusion. Indeed, this ambiguity emerges strikingly at

> Rightly to be great
> Is not to stir without great argument[.]

According to the main context, what Hamlet intends to express here is actually the opposite idea: that to be truly great you *should* 'stir without great argument'; but, in the line as he utters it, the 'not' negates that evidently-intended meaning and lets through the covert sense that one should require a very strong justification before taking arms. (To preserve the logical sense by adding another 'not' would create the grossly unmetrical line, 'Is *not* not to stir without great argument'.) So this passage offers an ambiguity which lies between William Empson's 'Fourth Type' (in which 'the alternative meanings combine to make clear a complicated state of mind') and the 'Seventh Type' (full contradiction).[2] There is even a further ambiguity, local and syntactical, which should delight Freudians: 'I . . . . . / That have a father kill'd, a mother stain'd'.

In short, although Hamlet reproaches himself for not emulating Fortinbras' army, he does so in terms which may lead the audience to conclude that he has better reason for hesitating than he recognises. Such layered utterances help to generate the sense that beneath Hamlet's avowed intentions and motives there lies a region of covert and contrasting intentions and motives. To postulate, then, subconscious or unconscious motivation for Hamlet is not to abuse the text or to confuse a fictional being with a real one; it is to make valid inferences from the text's own detailed ambiguities.

Laertes

As we have noted, the parallelism between Laertes and Hamlet is artfully established as early as Act I, scene ii, and begins soon after the discussion of the political problem offered by Fortinbras. Laertes, who has returned to Denmark for the coronation, now wishes to go back to France; this has his father's approval, and Claudius readily grants permission. Then we learn that Hamlet, who had evidently returned to Denmark for the funeral, also seeks permission—in his case, to go back to Wittenberg University; both Claudius and Gertrude urge him to stay, and he agrees to obey his mother. The Claudius who here urges Hamlet to remain will later be anxious to send him away, to England. In scene iii, Laertes, on the eve of departure, urges Ophelia not to trust Hamlet's courtship but to guard her chastity from the prince who is too far above her rank to be a potential husband. This advice prepares the way for Polonius' subsequent insistence that Ophelia should shun Hamlet—an insistence which will help to bring about Ophelia's subsequent suffering, madness and death.

In Act II, scene i, which evidently assumes a time-gap of about two months since the events of Act I, Polonius instructs Reynaldo to take money and messages to Laertes in Paris, and also to make crafty enquiries to discover whether Laertes is behaving respectably or is gaming, drinking, fencing, swearing or 'drabbing'. Thus Reynaldo may 'By indirections find directions out'. T. S. Eliot, echoing the claims of J. M. Robertson, remarked of Hamlet that 'there are unexplained scenes—the Polonius–Laertes and the Polonius–Reynaldo scenes—for which there is little excuse';[3] but, if 'excuse' be needed, it may be amply found not only in the clear establishment of the characters of Laertes and Polonius, who will be crucially important in the subsequent action, and not only in the fine realism of Polonius' meandering absentmindedness (II.i. 38–55), but also in the thematic and ironic functions of these exchanges. The ubiquitous theme of 'spies and spying' is strongly enriched by Act II, scene i: Polonius is here enthusiastically arranging to spy on Laertes, as he will soon arrange to spy on Hamlet; the theme of 'the older versus the younger generation', or, more precisely, of 'distrust and friction between the older and the younger generations', becomes amplified here; and the clause 'By indirections find directions out' has thematic value for the whole plot.

The strongest parallel between Laertes and Hamlet is, of
course, ironically established when Hamlet kills Polonius
while thinking he may be killing Claudius; thus a son who
laments the murder of his father acts precipitately in a way
which bereaves another son and provokes a further course
of vengeance. Claudius, whose murder of King Hamlet had
gone undetected by the public, now finds that he is widely
thought to be the murderer of Polonius; and Laertes' course
as an avenger makes an intricate ironic counterpoint to that
of the prince. At first, Laertes is impetuous and histrionic;
next, he is unctuously wooed by Claudius to pursue a
Machiavellian course, and to pursue it unhesitatingly:

>   That we would do,
> We should do when we would: for this 'would'
>   changes
> And hath abatements and delays as many
> As there are tongues, are hands, are accidents;
> And then this 'should' is like a spendthrift sigh
> That hurts by easing.

Here, the first irony is that Claudius echoes a warning
against inconstancy offered by the Player-King in the play
that Hamlet had chosen as a test of Claudius (III.ii. 180–92);
the second is that Claudius is providing, unwittingly, a
critical commentary on Hamlet's own self-conscious
indecision. Laertes says he'd be willing to cut Hamlet's
throat in church; and the Claudius who, while at prayer, had
been spared by the prince, now remarks, 'No place indeed
should murder sanctuarize; / Revenge should have no
bounds.' Claudius and Laertes then plan the means of
Hamlet's death: an unblunted and poisoned rapier (which
will, in the event, kill Laertes as well as Hamlet, and will
wound Claudius) together with a cup of poisoned wine
(which will, in a further ruthless irony, kill Gertrude and
despatch Claudius).

Act V, scene i, unites Hamlet, Laertes and the dead

Ophelia in a sequence of violent discords. Hamlet discovers tardily that the grave-digger with whom he has been discussing mortality has been digging the grave of 'the fair Ophelia' (to whom the queen says, 'I hop'd thou shouldst have been my Hamlet's wife') and that the chief mourner is Laertes, esteemed by Hamlet as 'a very noble youth'. Laertes offers a hyperbolic, almost hysterical lamentation; Hamlet challenges him; they grapple wildly in the very grave; and Hamlet (half in earnest, half in parody) rivals Laertes' melodramatic rhetoric with his own:

> Woo't weep, woo't fight, woo't fast, woo't tear
> thyself,
> Woo't drink up eisel, eat a crocodile?
> I'll do't. Dost come here to whine,
> To outface me with leaping in her grave?
> Be buried quick with her, and so will I.
> And if thou prate of mountains, let them throw
> Millions of acres on us, till our ground,
> Singeing his pate against the burning zone,
> Make Ossa like a wart. Nay, and thou'lt mouth,
> I'll rant as well as thou.

In that last sentence, there sounds the characteristic sardonic note, the awareness and intelligence of Hamlet— and also the characteristic realism of this text which, so often, places in a critical framework the large gestures and bold oratory that, a few years earlier in the history of drama, would have been offered uncritically. Again, the scene offers densely layered ironies. 'I lov'd you ever', says Hamlet to Laertes, whose father has been briskly slaughtered by the prince, and whose sister died as a consequence (in part) of Hamlet's rejection; 'I lov'd Ophelia', says the Hamlet who had treated Ophelia so harshly; and the two men (who might in other circumstances have been friends) now rant and wrestle in the grave—and over the very corpse—of the young woman whom they purport to be mourning, watched by the king whose murderous ambition is the origin of these discords and distresses, and mocked by a litter of bones and taciturn skulls.

The parallelism between Hamlet and Laertes is given fully explicit acknowledgement in Act V, scene ii:

> *Hamlet.*   But I am very sorry, good Horatio,
> That to Laertes I forgot myself;
> For by the image of my cause I see
> The portraiture of his. I'll court his favours.

And he proceeds to court the favours of Laertes by making a gallant, if not wholly truthful, apology to him when they meet for the duel. Laertes prosecutes the vengeful scheme ('And yet it is almost against my conscience'), and the multiple ironies of the dénouement unfold: the festive cannonades re-echo; Laertes and Claudius are caught in the trap they set for Hamlet (the 'Mousetrap' theme completed); Claudius' death is precipitated by Laertes' confession; Hamlet attains his revenge not by his own plotting so much as by his enemies' devices and sheer chance, as though to reinforce again both the maxim that 'There's a divinity that shapes our ends, / Rough-hew them how we will' and the Player-King's affirmation that 'Our thoughts are ours, their ends none of our own'; and Fortinbras, once another vengeful son, attains by 'election' the kingdom he formerly sought by violence.

Pyrrhus

In Act II, scene ii, Hamlet asks the First Player to recite a speech which the prince particularly loves: Aeneas' description of the slaughter of Priam by Pyrrhus, the Greek who was seeking to avenge his slain father, Achilles. The recitation tells how, at the sack of Troy, old Priam was hacked to pieces by the vengeful Pyrrhus, and how Priam's wife, Hecuba, made an 'instant burst of clamour'. The Player weeps in sympathy with the imagined Hecuba, and Hamlet subsequently reflects, in soliloquy, that if an actor can be so moved by fictional suffering, then Hamlet should be all the more moved to vengeful action by his knowledge of the real fate of the former king. In this sequence there is a powerful ambiguity which relates closely to that in the later soliloquy, 'How all occasions do inform against me' (IV.iv. 32–66). The player's recitation emphasises the horror of revenge: in this case, a black-clad, bloodstained and 'hellish' warrior, 'horridly trick'd / With blood of fathers, mothers, daughters, sons', slaughters a feeble old man ('mincing' the limbs) before the horrified gaze of the victim's wife. Though Hamlet derives from the recitation a rebuke to his inaction, what the audience derives is largely an entirely different sense: the nightmarish barbarism of the revenge ethic. From his stained armour ('o'ersized with coagulate gore') to his 'eyes like carbuncles', Pyrrhus is transformed from the human to the monstrous, and the emphasis on the age and feebleness of 'reverend Priam' accentuates the sense of moral indignation at the deed. And this is the passage that Hamlet 'chiefly loved' and likes to have recalled: a passage which speaks, as loudly as any passage could, against ruthless revenge. His choice may serve his indignation (Hecuba's distress exposes the equanimity of the bereaved Gertrude); but since Pyrrhus slew in revenge and Claudius did not, it inevitably gives the impression that at a subconscious level Hamlet is seeking vindication of delay rather than incentives to retribution. The evidence is there, solidly, in the text: Hamlet has chosen a passage which indicts revenge and does not justify it. The choice clearly exhibits intentionality (and whether it be conscious or unconscious is critically irrelevant);[4] imaginative intentionality on the part of an author, which in this case encourages also an imputation of imaginative intentionality to the fictional character.

THE DELAY

Hamlet repeatedly reproaches himself for his tardiness in avenging his father, and the ghost concurs. In Act III, scene iv, this exchange takes place:

> *Hamlet.*   Do you not come your tardy son to chide,
>   That, laps'd in time and passion, lets go by
>   Th'important acting of your dread
>   command?
>   O say.
> *Ghost.*   Do not forget. This visitation
>   Is but to whet thy almost blunted purpose.

This exchange occurs a short time after Hamlet's decision to refrain from murdering Claudius while he is at prayer, and within a few minutes of the killing of Polonius, whom Hamlet had seemingly mistaken for the king ('I took thee for thy better'). How, then, can we reconcile the ghost's authoritative statement that Hamlet's purpose is 'almost blunted' with Hamlet's avowed intention to kill Claudius not while he is at prayer but in circumstances which will ensure the king's damnation? The obvious and traditional mode of reconciliation is to infer that the avowal was really self-deception, a rationalisation of delay by someone with an inner resistance to the murder of a defenceless man. This congenial explanation appears to fit neatly; and that the ghost's reproachful reappearance occurs during Hamlet's passionate upbraiding of his mother permits the easy inference that Hamlet's treatment here of Gertrude is not germane to the cause of revenge but indicates a conflict between that cause and the prince's bitter preoccupation with Gertrude's sexuality. This, however, makes more acute the problem of reconciling the ghost's (and Hamlet's) sense of a neglected task with the fact that Hamlet has, a few minutes ago, killed a man whom he had apparently mistaken for Claudius. One way of dealing with this problem is to say

that when the prince thrust his rapier through the arras he
was striking wildly, reflexively, without premeditation, not
knowing at that instant who might be there:

Polonius. [*behind the arras*] What ho! Help!
Hamlet.   How now? A rat! Dead for a ducat, dead.
              [*Thrusts his rapier through the arras.*]
Polonius. [*behind*] O, I am slain.
Queen.   O me, what hast thou done?
Hamlet.   Nay, I know not.
              Is it the King?

Thus, although Hamlet later says of the dead Polonius, 'I
took thee for thy better', this is again rationalisation; at the
moment of the killing, Hamlet was striking blindly, as is
witnessed by his 'Nay, I know not'. The murderous action
can thus be reconciled with the ghost's reproach; for,
though lethal, it was not 'purpos'd' as a killing of Claudius.
Once again, however, we are supplying explanations to a
part of the text which is reticent; and the very reticence
which generates our quest for an explanation (we seek to
speak on behalf of the dumb text) also denies our
explanation a clinching proof; it is as though this same
muteness implies a sardonic reproach of this kind: 'Given
that elsewhere *Hamlet* is so informatively loquacious, why,
if your interpretation is right, should it here be so strikingly
reticent?'
     In revenge dramas, one obvious basis of suspense is the
audience's interest in the manner by which vengeance will
be achieved: how will the avenger go about his task,
overcoming external opposition? In *Hamlet*, Shakespeare
develops a subtler principle of suspense (which had been
displayed far less intriguingly in Aeschylus' Orestes and
Kyd's Hieronymo): will the avenger actually *shirk* his task?
Hamlet is quite as active as most revengers; what is new is
not that he berates himself for the delay (Hieronymo had
also done so) but that he seeks and fails to determine the

reason for it; indeed, he forestalls many an interpreter by asserting that he has 'cause, and will, and strength, and means' to accomplish the deed. As William Empson pointed out, this generates a novel psychological interest: audiences are encouraged to speculate about (and thus to generate) a mysteriously deep inner self of the hero. At least as important is that Shakespeare has found a novel way of co-ordinating a plot which often reflects the seeming vagrancy of real life. If a hero, from time to time, says 'I'm neglecting the important task', this is an excellent way of reminding the audience of that task and thus linking to the main plot the customary peripheral intrigues, complications and retarding-devices which enable the drama to be sustained to full length. What is normally quite traditional and unproblematic (the fact that the road to the dénouement must be a tortuous road) is here made conspicuous and problematic; the protagonist, by saying 'This wasn't relevant to the goal', sets up a novel tension between the customary complications and the simple basis of the dramatic action.

So, although psychological and moral explanations of the delay are tempting and largely plausible, the technical explanation has the merit of being less speculative. Shakespeare has, in any case, anticipated the twentieth-century taste for literary lacunae which can be vindicated by theories about human opacity or the 'decentred' self. The term 'delayed decoding' (coined by Ian Watt)[5] refers to those literary sequences in which the author specifies a puzzling effect while retarding or withholding an explanation of its cause; and in Joseph Conrad's characterisations, such delayed decoding occasionally serves to emphasise the opacity of a character's inner nature. The main cognitive value of Shakespeare's dramatisation of Hamlet's introspections on delay is that they memorably express a familiar dilemma of modern civilised people. The reflective capacity which gives the individual a strong sense of unique selfhood does so by establishing a critical distance

not only between the self and the world but also between the
conscious mind and the ulterior regions of the self (as well as
the physical body). Hamlet's perplexity may be a means to
an end, which is not the discovery of a reason for his
procrastination but rather the dramatising of the paradox
that the seeming guarantor of selfhood, the reflective mind,
is also its belittling betrayer. For those who seek thematic
co-ordination, there are few aspects of Hamlet which are not
co-ordinated by this paradox.

Hamlet sums it up (characteristically effecting a collision
of stereotypes) when he says:

> What piece of work is a man, how noble in reason, how
> infinite in faculties, in form and moving how express and
> admirable; in action how like an angel, in apprehension
> how like a god: the beauty of the world, the paragon of
> animals—and yet, to me, what is this quintessence of
> dust?

AN EXPERIMENT IN REALISM?

Although a brief plot-summary might suggest that Hamlet
belonged to the genre of revenge drama, to term the play 'a
revenge drama' seems demeaning. One obvious reason for
this is that Shakespeare, by giving subtly and even
ostentatiously realistic treatment to what he inherited as a
revenge play, has provided the ethical complexity and the
problematic embodiment which have subsequently become
widely accepted as defining characteristics of a tragedy.

In the revenge dramas which were so popular in England
between 1580 and 1640, a conspicuous plot-pattern (which
prevails in some famous examples, though certainly not in
all) is as follows. A protagonist with whom we have
sympathy is shocked by the murder of some relative or
loved one; being unable to secure justice through normal
legal channels (perhaps because the authorities are corrupt),

he pursues a scheme of private vengeance against the wrong-
doer, and eventually accomplishes his revenge—but it is
usually the case that the avenger himself perishes as a
consequence of the scheme. The customary explanation of
the popularity of such dramas is plausible, though it over-
simplifies the spectators' responses: the audience's rational
sense that the taking of private revenge is morally wrong and
socially dangerous (forbidden by church and state; open to
abuse; a threat to order) is gratified by the protagonist's
death; but the audience's emotional sympathy with the
protagonist is gratified by the success of his vindictive
scheme, and the sympathy will be the stronger according to
the lack of available means of legal redress, the suffering
borne by the protagonist, and the vileness of his foe. The
audience gains theatrical excitement from the vicarious
experience of ingenious and ruthless action, together with
the further satisfaction of seeing how the avenger is yet
imperilled or destroyed as a result of his own devices. Both
primitive and civilised moral feelings are thus evoked and
gratified. The attraction of the revenge plot is demonstrated
by its resilience down the centuries: in the twentieth
century, countless western films, crime films, televised
melodramas and popular thrillers have used the basic plot-
pattern of revenge drama, though there has been a tendency
for the avenging protagonist to escape death, albeit
narrowly. For numerous writers, a crucial problem is that of
enabling the hero to take bloody revenge on the villain
without thereby incurring the moral obloquy that would
normally be incurred by a killer. Shakespeare found a
solution which is still being zealously employed by
playwrights and script-writers today: the hero kills in rapid,
almost reflexive, reaction after finding that he has walked
into a lethal ambush set by the villain. Furthermore, *Hamlet*
reflects the still-current sentimental fantasy that the man of
sensitivity may be able to defeat the men of violence on their
own terms.

Fredson Bowers, seeking to explain the popularity of

revenge drama among Elizabethans, has emphasised that at a time when, for political reasons (the need to preserve the status quo and to avert the danger of civil war), church and state sought to outlaw private revenge, there would have remained a strong undercurrent of sympathy for the person who acts as an avenger, particularly when vengeance is sought for the death of a parent, wife or child.[6] We can understand that 'undercurrent' readily, since it still flows through public attitudes today: when news items tell us of especially brutal or callous crimes, we may often feel that the judicial sentence is inappropriately lenient. One historic reason for the popularity of revenge dramas around 1600 was the audience's knowledge of the ingenious and ruthless revenges which had actually taken place in Spain, France and the Renaissance Italy of the Borgias; indeed, for writers in officially Protestant England it was ideologically prudent to associate Roman Catholic lands with corruption and intrigue. Another reason for their popularity was subtler: revenge dramas were a meeting-point of ideological orthodoxy and subversion. Machiavelli had written, 'In the actions of all men (and especially of princes), where there is no tribunal to which we can appeal, we judge by results.'[7] Often the avenger lacks a *legal* tribunal to which he can appeal; but his actions could sometimes imply the perilous excitements of a time when there might be no *divine* tribunal either, so that man would become the sole moral arbiter. In the fiction, orthodoxy might eventually be vindicated; yet the centrality of the avenger leaves no doubt that it was in the morally incursionary and subversive features of the action that much of the dramatic interest lay. What the relative realism of *Hamlet* permitted was, among other things, a very elaborate evocation of the ethical and religious questioning which revenge drama often suggested but seldom evoked with such persuasive and engaging intelligence. Its interrogative potentiality was realised. Hamlet never says 'Revenge is wrong', and he often talks and behaves as though it is right; but the play's network of parallelisms and juxtapositions, its system of comparisons and its varied human textures, all give the topic of revenge and its implications a very thorough interrogation.

We know that Shakespeare's *Hamlet* was based on a previous play which appeared in the late 1580s. We also know that in the decade between then and the emergence of Shakespeare's version, the drama was evolving from stylisation towards realism. This process of evolution, irregular, fluctuating, but clear enough in its general direction, can readily be traced in Shakespeare's work during that period. The point is made most obviously by the contrast between *Hamlet* and the earlier *Titus Andronicus*, with its cumbersome rhetoric, formalised orations and lamentations, and its almost ludicrously barbaric violence. *Hamlet*, in a multiplicity of ways, conveys the sense of complicated, familiar modern life opposing archaic, simpler, more stylised modes; its realism lies largely in its seeming waywardness, its accommodation of material which does not seem requisite for the purposes of conventional plotting, and in its dramatisation of unconventional uncertainties. Part of this 'waywardness' may be accidental; but the extent of the ironic linkages in the play suggests that Shakespeare is already exploring the principle which was to be perfected by Ibsen in plays like *The Wild Duck* and *Hedda Gabler:* that of furthering the plot by means of material which initially seems digressive or trivial, and which can only in retrospect be seen as functional.

Subverted Stereotypes

One reason why audiences are able to sympathise with Hamlet's confused procrastination is that they can see that the court in which Hamlet moves does not have the stylised features of the conventional 'corrupt court' of revenge drama. In earlier and later revenge plays, a corrupt ruler tends to be markedly more wicked, lustful and generally obnoxious than is Claudius. The Claudius whom we see is so competent as ruler that we may feel that Hamlet is, at times, a cat among the pigeons. A king should command loyalty; Claudius does so: there is no doubt of his ability to secure the willing co-operation of Polonius, Laertes, Cornelius, Voltemand and the others. Even if he's only playing the part of a rightful king, he does so with skill and panache; he is adept at the authoritative yet diplomatically courteous speech. A good king should endeavour to ensure the security of his subjects—and that's exactly what Claudius does by the wise diplomacy which averts Fortinbras' invasion of Denmark; indeed, one of the functions of the play's initial emphasis on the threat to Denmark seems to be to stress Claudius' efficient propriety in statecraft. Later, we see that though he has murdered the rightful king, at least he is capable of feeling remorse; and even if the words of his prayer fly up while his thoughts remain below, he has still made the effort to express penitence to God. Commentators who would vindicate Hamlet's range of callous actions seek to exaggerate the corruption of the court in which he moves; but, compared with the courts of Macbeth or of Goneril and Regan, the court of Claudius is a passably civilised place; there is not the sense that is generated in Macbeth or in King Lear of metaphysical evil burgeoning, of turmoil in the elements, of horses devouring each other and storms wreaking havoc as a consequence of human immorality. Gertrude may have committed adultery with Claudius (she appears to concede this at III.iv. 88–91), but she's not the lascivious, lecherous consort of revenge drama; compared with, say, the grotesquely randy Duchess in Tourneur's Revenger's Tragedy, she seems a decent, maternally worried person: she's worried by Hamlet's apparent madness, saddened by Ophelia's death, and anxious to reconcile Claudius and her son. She tells a defensive lie when reporting to Claudius what Hamlet said in her chamber; she excuses Hamlet to

Laertes after the struggle in the graveyard; and the affection
between Claudius and Gertrude is so strong that Claudius is
prepared to expose his own scheming by his vain endeavour
to prevent her drinking from the poisoned cup. 'Something
is rotten in the state of Denmark': but the state is not as
rotten as we initially expect; indeed, it is a state in which
traditional decencies are conspicuously preserved: the
discussions, early on, between Ophelia, Laertes and
Polonius seem almost expressly designed to say: 'This is no
Italianate court of lust and seething ambition; this is a court
with familiar concerns for virtue, propriety, prudence,
reputation and common sense'.

All this partly explains the complex appeal of the play to
audiences. When Hamlet reproaches himself for not
pursuing revenge, part of us can endorse the reproaches—
not simply the part of us that is sympathetic to the primitive
view that the murder of a father justifies bloody private
revenge, but also the 'aesthetic' side of us which relishes the
act of revenge as an exciting stage-spectacle; and yet, when
Hamlet appears to delay, we can understand such a delay
partly on ethical and pragmatic grounds; we observe that
this court does not contain stereotyped villainy. And one
source of Hamlet's anguish is that he senses this fact and
strives to overcome it by force of rhetoric. The more
Hamlet upbraids his mother for 'honeying and making love
/ Over the nasty sty' and for craving 'the rank sweat of an
enseamèd bed', the more we recognise a histrionic excess of
vividly experienced disgust; though she says that he has
'cleft [her] heart in twain', nothing that she says or does fully
confirms his view of her as lust-besotted. Similarly, when
Hamlet (before he knows of the murder as well as
afterwards) vehemently contrasts the noble King Hamlet
('Hyperion') and the ignoble Claudius ('a satyr'), he seems to
be attempting to make life simpler than it is: the late king is
described in terms which depict him as too faultless to be
credible (and the ghost acknowledges its burden of human
sins), while Claudius is described in terms which seem to

offer a conventional caricature of villainy—an image too crude to tally with the Claudius whom we see. We can understand why Hamlet would wish to simplify and clarify his emotions by translating his father, Gertrude and Claudius into stereotypes (we are all tempted by this process when seeking to bolster or facilitate our emotional lives), but understanding does not entail endorsement.

The ghost had sought to impose a stereotype on Hamlet— that of the dedicated avenger—but Hamlet had found within himself an obscure resistance to the conventional role. In trying to conform to the ghost's expectations, Hamlet strives to impose stereotypes on others; but the reality proves critically recalcitrant. The slain Polonius is scorned by the prince as a 'wretched, rash, intruding fool'; yet Polonius had meant well: he had hidden in Gertrude's chamber in order to discover the cause of Hamlet's apparent madness and thereby to seek a cure; and had Hamlet not behaved in so provocatively strange a manner, Polonius would not have needed to eavesdrop. Later, seeking to exculpate his readiness to send Rosencrantz and Guildenstern to their deaths, Hamlet says to Horatio, 'Why, man, they did make love to this employment': but nothing in the text proves that they were aware that the letter from Claudius to the English king included Hamlet's death-warrant; their culpability (though likely) is never confirmed. This central opacity redeems them from their stereotyping as interchangeably obsequious functionaries and vindicates their transtextual resurrection in the theatre of Tom Stoppard.

Some of the strongest ironies in the play are generated by the subversion of the conventional rhetoric concerning royal power. In III.iii. 15–23, Rosencrantz assures Claudius that the 'cess of majesty' causes a 'boist'rous ruin' and 'general groan': one irony being that, as Claudius knows well, the smooth succession following the sudden death of King Hamlet has belied that hyperbolic view of the importance of the ruler. The irony is redoubled when

Claudius, whose murder of King Hamlet had gone undetected, is thought by the people to be the murderer of Polonius; and, told of their rebellion, Claudius utters the stock piety which his own success as usurper refutes:

> There's such divinity doth hedge a king
> That treason can but peep to what it would,
> Acts little of his will.

Perhaps the most conspicuous and dramatically painful instance of the conflict between stereotype and reality comes when Hamlet (III.i.) seeks to impose on Ophelia the misogynist's image of wanton womanhood at large:

> [T]he power of beauty will sooner transform honesty from what it is to a bawd than the force of honesty can translate beauty into his likeness ..... You jig and amble, you lisp, you nickname God's creatures, and make your wantonness your ignorance.

(He has it both ways by saying that even if she were chaste she would not escape calumny.) The misogynistic diatribe is a common ingredient of revenge drama; but in *Hamlet* the context denounces it. Ophelia, repeatedly a victim of masculine manipulation, is patently and poignantly innocent; Hamlet's verbal aggression (poison in the ear) helps to bring about her eventual derangement and death; her ecstasy of dementia is a protest against the egoistic harshness of his feigned madness, while her self-destruction is a protest against his calumnious project.

Hamlet himself does indeed sound, at times, like the stereotypical avenger (notably in III.ii. 379–83):

> 'Tis now the very witching time of night,
> When churchyards yawn and hell itself breathes out
> Contagion to this world. Now could I drink hot
>   blood,

And do such bitter business as the day
Would quake to look on.

A related instance is his avowed determination (III.iii.
73–96) to kill Claudius not at prayer but in circumstances
which will ensure 'that his soul may be . . . . . damn'd'.
Such conventionally vengeful speeches contrast so strongly
with the introspective sensitivity and humanity which
Hamlet displays elsewhere that readers are usually
reluctant, as we have seen, to take his words at face value; in
the former case they may think that Hamlet is simply
attempting to 'talk himself into' a conventional attitude: in
the latter case they may argue (with some confirmation from
the ghost's subsequent rebuke) that Hamlet is rationalising
his delay. Nevertheless, he acts out the revenger's role
vigorously enough in killing Polonius and despatching
Rosencrantz and Guildenstern. So the reader may postulate
a 'manic-depressive' Hamlet, to account for his variability
and partly to exculpate him; or the reader may point out that
alongside the magnanimous, friendly and thoughtful
Hamlet there exists an arrogant Prince Hamlet whose
aristocratic sense of the social inferiority of others makes
him the less concerned about their lives: 'I took thee for thy
better', he says of Polonius; and of Rosencrantz and
Guildenstern:

'Tis dangerous when the baser nature comes
Between the pass and fell incensèd points
Of mighty opposites.

He also displays an increasing ability to exculpate himself by
regarding his bloodier actions as the manifestations of
God's will. In the case of Polonius,

heaven hath pleas'd it so
To punish me with this and this with me[;]

while, in the case of Rosencrantz and Guildenstern, 'a divinity' is at work, so that even in the detail of the seal-ring 'was heaven ordinant'. It's characteristic of *Hamlet* that this confidence in divine ordinance should be expressed by the prince who said, 'There is nothing either good or bad but thinking makes it so', and whose meditations in the cemetery had offered the powerfully sceptical sense that pagan and Christian, 'Imperious Caesar' and 'poor Yorick' alike, must end in dust and clay. What makes Hamlet so seductive and so baffling to interpreters is largely that Shakespeare, experimenting in realistically complex characterisation, lets Hamlet invoke, animate and traverse different stereotypes without solidifying into a stereotype himself. He is consistent in his ability to crystallise heterogeneous possibilities, and the play is consistent in its quality of purposeful volatility which necessarily eludes orthodox demonstrations of consistency. As stereotypical array is fragmented into realistic disarray, so ideological order is fragmented into ideological contradiction—until the concluding ironic rearrangement. When Hamlet at last abandons the endeavour to impose stereotyped roles upon himself and his society (entering the duel in a coolly fatalistic mood), then, as Claudius and—for a while—Laertes become Machiavells, muddle resolves itself into climax, dénouement and closure, and countless details of the previous action interlock in a seemingly inevitable sequence. The festive carousals and cannonades of the wedding celebrations in Act I re-echo as the carousals and cannonades which proclaim retribution upon the poisoner of King Hamlet. 'Is thy union here?', the prince asks Claudius, as the 'union' becomes at once the pearl, the poison, a remarriage with Gertrude in the night of death, and the merging of injustice into justice. Even the random coincidences of the plot (the incursion of the pirates, the exchange of rapiers, the intercepted wine-cup) have all fulfilled the prophetic maxim of the Player-King:

But orderly to end where I begun,
Our wills and fates do so contrary run
That our devices still are overthrown:
Our thoughts are ours, their ends none of our own.

The most cunning structural strategy of *Hamlet* has been
the deployment of a doctrine which enables the fortuitous
to be interpreted as the providential. Alexander Pope was to
epitomise it: 'All Chance, Direction, which thou canst
not see.'[8] The ingeniously ironic closure of the plot has
invoked as its philosophical lubricant an appropriately
ironic theological doctrine: Fortune, who maintains the
appearances of unjust disorder in this world, thereby serves
the just order of God. 'There's a divinity that shapes our
ends'; 'We defy augury. There is special providence in the
fall of a sparrow . . . . . The readiness is all.'

ACTORS, ACTING AND ACTION

If there be any doubt that *Hamlet* is largely an experiment in
realism, we have only to consider the centrality to the play
of the advice given by the prince to the players in Act III,
scene ii. Don't mouth the speeches, he says, don't rant or
saw the air:

> Suit the action to the word, the word to the action, with
> this special observance, that you o'erstep not the
> modesty of nature. For anything so o'erdone is from the
> purpose of playing, whose end, both at the first and now,
> was and is to hold as 'twere the mirror up to nature; to
> show virtue her feature, scorn her own image, and the
> very age and body of the time his form and pressure.

What Hamlet says here has become so famous, so
frequently quoted, and seems so clear in its gist, that its
implication for the whole play may be overlooked. Hamlet

is asking for realism. He's opposed to rant, ham-acting, bombast and self-indulgence; the play should hold 'the mirror up to nature'—reflect reality. This idea of acting as an imitation of life is traditional and as ancient as Aristotle's *Poetics*, but Hamlet's gloss on the ancient idea gives it detail and precision. So any director of *Hamlet* is thus given clear guidance about the mode which should predominate in a stage-production. And the main action's realism is, of course, heightened by the contrast with the conspicuous stylisation of (in turn) the First Player's recitation about Pyrrhus, the mime of *The Murder of Gonzago*, and the spoken part of that play-within-the-play. The recitation proclaims a style of verse which would have seemed up-to-date in 1590 but which by 1600 was ponderously rhetorical; and the arthritic pentameter of the double play-within-the-play again heightens, by contrast, the prevailing realism of the main action, while Hamlet's advice to the players makes us the more suspicious of histrionic utterances by major characters. (The suspicions are confirmed when Hamlet shouts at the furious Laertes, 'I'll rant as well as thou'.) One consequence is that in this drama, to a greater degree than in other tragedies of Shakespeare, it is difficult for us to distinguish confidently between impassioned utterance, histrionic self-dramatisation and deceptive display. Furthermore, a higher proportion of Hamlet's speeches is in prose (and a shrewdly lively, colloquial prose) than is the case with other Shakespearian tragic heroes—hence, in part, his 'modernity'.

Thus the theme of 'actors and acting' becomes another of the co-ordinating features of the play. Claudius is a usurper who acts the part of a rightful king. The itinerant players are victims of usurpation (II.ii. 335–64). The ghost may (Hamlet reflects) be a devil acting the part of King Hamlet; the costume it chooses is a suit of armour, reminding us grimly of the combat in which the Danish king had slain Old Fortinbras. Polonius had performed the role of Caesar, and was stabbed in play as he will be stabbed in reality. One court entertainment is designed to ambush Claudius; another is designed to ambush the prince. The fatal duel is prompted by a visitor called Lamord, a name which sounds like that of Death (La Mort) in disguise. The Player-King, from within his theatrical make-up and trudging rhetoric, seems to be commenting sardonically on both Claudius and Hamlet. Hamlet himself plays the fool, feigning madness; yet, in his harsh and hysterical moments, we may suspect that the feigned madness disguises a real neurosis. And when central figures are acting out roles, the theme of spying, eavesdropping and testing is entailed: people spy on each other to seek the truth behind the masks. Ghost, Claudius, Polonius, Rosencrantz and Guildenstern spy on Hamlet; he, in various ways, spies on them; and his own recessive inner nature seems to elude focused perception by himself or anyone else.

Furthermore, as *Hamlet* has moved through time to the present, becoming a renowned classic of the theatre, a new paradox has developed. This play, which (by Elizabethan standards) wields such remarkable realism, has become so well known that its most spontaneous-seeming and interestingly unconventional features have also become parts of a time-hallowed ritual. The apparently fortuitous is now the predictably inexorable; the freest Hamlet is the most convincingly captivated by the role. But although the work's innovatory radicalism has become institutionalised, the institutionalised work may become, in any new stage-version, radically rejuvenated. Politically, the plot has some obviously conservative features: the usurper who killed a monarch meets his nemesis; the prince (though guilty of murder) receives eulogies; and no suggestion is offered that the rulers of a state should be other than a small élite. Structurally, it offers the fraudulent 'consolation' of literary tragedies: whereas in reality death may strike casually in Act I (a child crushed by a car in the street) or sardonically in Act XI (a senile woman expiring in a geriatric ward), in tragedies death hospitably accords its victim the climactic significance of Act V. The radicalism of *Hamlet* lies not in the paraphrasable plot but in the embodiment; in the quality of searching, questioning articulacy.

·3·

'There has been much to do on both sides':
Various Findings

PROBLEMS FOR SOLUTION OR
DISSOLUTION?

We may now review and relinquish a familiar cluster of problems: (1) Hamlet's delay; (2) the apparent inconsistency between his civilised nature and his brutal actions; and (3) that he seems more obsessed by the treacherous sexuality of Gertrude than by the murderous turpitude of Claudius.

Hamlet asks himself why he is slow to kill Claudius, and speculates that one explanation may be a habit of 'thinking too precisely on th'event'; but neither he nor anyone else in the play produces a final answer. Shakespeare may well have had no answer either, but what is certain is that he chose to emphasise the notion of the enigmatic delay. The self-interrogation strengthens the characterisation of Hamlet as a pioneer of modern introspective selfhood, while reminding us of the plot-direction; indeed, we have seen that the self-questioning soliloquies of Act II, scene ii, and Act IV, scene iv, function partly as bridges whereby the dramatic complications which must necessarily be deployed (in order to prevent a premature dénouement in a brisk assassination at the end of Act I) can be connected to the main plot which cannot be completed until Act V. The

effect of the frustrated self-enquiry is to generate the sense of
a deep, inaccessible region in Hamlet's nature; an excellent
strategy for creating the illusion of a complex real person. In
everyday life we may often be baffled when we fail to do
something which we believe we ought to do; in the dramas
of Shakespeare's day, it was unusual for someone to probe
so unavailingly in this way: hence our recognition that a new
realism was thus entering both the theatre and the definition
of the human. What Hamlet's soliloquies specify (or
suggest) very clearly is a quality of opacity in his nature.
Commentators, perplexed by that opacity, long sought to
convert it into a transparency through which some
explanatory factor could be discerned; and we have seen
various examples of such conversions—some quite
plausible, none fully verifiable. That sense of perplexity,
however, should by now be dwindling, for obvious cultural
reasons. One of the most characteristic features of
modernist literature has been its emphasis on the opacity of
individuals. In Conrad's Lord Jim and Mister Kurtz, in
Mann's Aschenbach, in Woolf's Mrs Ramsay, and
repeatedly in the writings of Kafka, Sartre and Camus, what
is emphasised (virtually to the point of cliché) is that an
individual may centrally be opaque not only to others but
also to himself or herself. The assumption of many past
commentators on *Hamlet* was that if a character asks a big
question about his own nature, the text is obliged to supply
the answer. But one of the notions propagated by modernist
literature and its advocates was that the function of such a
question may be to draw attention to the absence of an
accessible answer—indeed, to the fact of human opacity. So
the mystery of Hamlet's 'delay' may fade, if only because we
are increasingly willing to acknowledge the valid
deployment in literature of such inexplicability. Joseph
Conrad said in 1912, 'The part of the inexplicable should be
allowed for in appraising the conduct of men in a world
where no explanation is final';[1] and recent theorists have
emphasised that once we have peeled from the human self

the layers imposed by ideology, hardly anything remains for inspection.

The second item was the difficulty of explaining how Hamlet, who is so highly civilised, can also be capable of bloody, brutal and callous action. Historical events in the twentieth century mock this alleged problem. Hitler's accomplices in barbaric and genocidal schemes included highly educated and sophisticated scientists, businessmen, officers, technicians, academics, doctors; the paradox of 'brutality within civilisation' is a patent historical fact. Twentieth-century 'culture' itself, in novels, plays and films, has accustomed us to the notion that a 'heroic' protagonist may display reflective scruples but yet be capable of acting violently and cynically. One need be no Freudian but merely an observer of history to accept the principle that within a rational and sophisticated individual may lurk a readiness to assault and kill. In Hamlet, such a readiness co-exists with the sense that his resolution is 'sicklied o'er with the pale cast of thought'; but citizens whose elected leaders make zealous preparations for nuclear holocausts while simultaneously protracting labyrinthine negotiations to secure peace are not in a strong position to criticise Hamlet for inconsistency. Hamlet is indeed a palimpsest, a conglomerate of layered and opposed cultural accretions; but so are we.

To J. M. Robertson and T. S. Eliot, it appeared that Shakespeare's interest in dramatising Hamlet's disgust at his mother's sexuality conflicted with the requirements of the inherited revenge-plot. We have seen that, for Shakespeare, the multiple connotations of the term 'appetite' (unlawful political ambition, excessive consumption, and sexual greed) provided the imaginative co-ordinator. We have also seen that if Hamlet 'doth protest too much' when denouncing Gertrude and praising his father as a 'Hyperion', this is partly because the remarriage implies that the late king was not so peerless, and Claudius not so contemptible; therefore Hamlet strives to prop one stereotype by another

and another. The *Mousetrap* catches Hamlet: he wishes
Claudius and Gertrude to see themselves reflected in the
stylised treacherous couple of that performance; but
inevitably, for us, the effect is not only of similitude but also
of difference. The magnified gestures and stiff rhetoric of the
inner play emphasise the complicated realism of the outer
action. The life of *Hamlet* lies largely in its vigorous yet
critical and ironic deployment of the stereotypes; we are
engaged by the way in which the plot and its characters so
frequently slip away from the expected directions, the
predictable attitudes. Indeed, this ironic treatment is so
strong that it may make us more resistant than we would
normally be to the traditional features of the conclusion, its
epitomes and obituary tributes. Horatio proposes to sum
up the plot:

> So shall you hear
> Of carnal, bloody, and unnatural acts,
> Of accidental judgments, casual slaughters,
> Of deaths put on by cunning and forc'd cause,
> And, in this upshot, purposes mistook
> Fall'n on th'inventors' heads.

When he utters those words, we may well respond, 'Yes,
but it didn't seem so; what interested us was much less
summarisable'; and when Fortinbras says that Hamlet, had
he become ruler, 'was likely . . . . . / To have prov'd most
royal', something in us may well reply, 'Perhaps, but I doubt
it; and it wasn't a prospective "most royal" Hamlet that
interested us so much'. We enjoyed the action's novel
tension between the centripetal and the centrifugal, and
relished the opportunism with which the plot served as a
pretext for the interrogation of selfhood, reflection and
mortality.

   In the nineteenth century, critics usually accepted the
principle that if *Hamlet* could be proved to be coherent, it
thereby gained, and if it could be proved to be incoherent, it

lost prestige. In the late twentieth century, post-structuralists and deconstructionists often advocated (in their paradoxically orderly works) the principle that order in human affairs is merely a matter of ideological convention and imposition, and therefore gave a warm welcome to texts which seemed, by a quality of disorderliness, to support their scepticism. To such theorists the anomalies and contradictions of Hamlet were congenial, while the culmination of the action in ceremonialised closure was an embarrassment. Those critics, too, advocated a set of clichés (e.g., that empirical knowledge and common sense are ideological impositions, or that there is no essential human nature) which Hamlet both suggests and challenges.

The problem of overcoming the play's resistance to co-ordinating interpretations is one generated largely by the conditions of academic analysis of Hamlet as written text; in the theatre, as we shall see in the next section, the problem usually dissolves.

DIFFERENCES BETWEEN HAMLET ON THE PAGE AND ON THE STAGE

The long tradition which encouraged readers to regard a great literary work as 'an organic whole', the modern interest in 'close reading' (giving minute attention to details of imagery, ambiguity, etc.), and a sense of the venerable sanctity of the Shakespearian text, naturally encourage the studious reader to feel that a proper production of Hamlet should offer the full text, without excision; for how should we presume to know better than Shakespeare?

The first difficulty, as we have seen, is that there may be considerable disagreement about what the 'full text' is, given the differences between Q1, Q2 and F. The second difficulty is that 'Hamlet, in a conflation of the second Quarto and the Folio texts, would last over five hours':[2] so, in kindness to the toiling actors and in deference to the practical

economics of the theatre (save time, save money; axe a
character, trim the wage-bill), directors almost always cut
the text. One distinguished director, Trevor Nunn, has said:

> When you approach the text of *Hamlet*, the cutting
> virtually is the production. What you decide to leave in is
> your version of the play . . . . . Not only do I think cutting
> necessary, but (unfortunately) it can become extremely
> enjoyable . . . . . [M]y loyalty to the text is total, because it
> is my starting point and my finishing point. But I am not a
> fundamentalist about the text, because my prime concern
> *must* be to make the plays work in a theatre to an audience
> living now. Therefore if I have to make cuts, if I have to
> make elisions, if I have to telescope, even—dare I say it—
> in certain limited circumstances, expand, I will do so.[3]

Such statements may offend the scholarly purist; it is
unlikely that they would have offended Shakespeare, who,
as an actor and commercial playwright, was well aware that
the script is the negotiable basis for live performances and is
constantly open to revision in the light of changing
theatrical circumstances.

Clearly, a staged version of *Hamlet* will be influenced by
the prejudices and preoccupations of the director, the
capacities of the actors, the physical and financial amenities,
and the presumed interests of the audience; there is no such
thing as a 'neutral' production. On the other hand, the
grosser the liberties taken with the text, the more the
production should, in honesty, be advertised as a director's
free adaptation, or a new play 'based on' *Hamlet*, rather than
as Shakespeare's play. The most intelligent innovatory
versions of Shakespeare are usually those in which the
maximum plausible change of emphasis has been achieved
with the minimum alteration to the traditional text. In the
case of *Hamlet*, however, the 'traditional text' has long been
treated as an excessively lengthy script which, for theatrical
purposes, requires vigorous directorial editing; so the play

is more protean than most of Shakespeare's works, and the audience may find that Reynaldo is absent, or Osric, or even Fortinbras. And the peculiar complexity of Hamlet's character gives special attractiveness to the work as a stage-play: one actor might emphasise the noble and melancholy prince; another, the Oedipal neurotic; another, the apathetic student. Of David Warner's Hamlet (in the mid-1960s), one director reported:

> [T]he image of Hamlet as an apathetic, alienated graduate student provoked considerable reaction from those accustomed to the Renaissance prince. The younger generation took very much to *their* Hamlet. Here a production crystallised a generational division . . . . .[4]

Another director, Jonathan Miller, offers this summing-up:

> We will never be, and no one ever has been, introduced to Hamlet. I think of Hamlet as a series of lines to which an infinite series of claimants arrives and competes for . . . . . Hamlet is someone who might be someone, were there to be someone to claim him, and I think the job of rehearsal is to create a circumstance in which claimants will present themselves for examination.[5]

It's a pity that more of the professional critics and scholars have not adopted Miller's kind of openness; for, whereas those critics and scholars have so long pursued the mirage of the fully-explicable or 'essential' Hamlet, directors are far more likely to think in terms of an interesting 'possible' or 'viable' Hamlet. The approaches of both the critics and the directors are strongly dialectical, in that all of them are learning from and reacting against the conceptions of various predecessors; but in the theatrical world there is a frank, unembarrassed and indeed cordial recognition that Hamlet is 'a series of lines' welcoming 'an infinite series of claimants'. Different productions offer fruitfully conflicting co-ordinations.

One of the most obvious and striking effects of a good stage-production of *Hamlet* is that it vigorously elbows aside many of the doubts and problems that beset the scrupulous reader of the printed page. When we study the text privately, our responses tend to be more reflectively analytical; we have the opportunity to pause, consider, thumb back through the pages, and worry over inconsistencies and anomalies. The stage-production is a succession of vivid present moments; the immediate dominates our vision. Some classic plays command *respect* as eloquent rituals; *Hamlet*, on the other hand, has a peculiar ability to evoke and retain our inquisitive *interest*. This results partly from the variety of attitudes within Hamlet himself, and from the variety of strongly defined roles around him; it's partly a matter of the play's structure of parallels and contrasts. There's a wide range of tones, of diverse kinds of eloquence, from the Player-King's stiffly histrionic majesty to the grave-digger's jaunty ruminations, while the prince's wit shimmers as brief rainbows in the spray flung by rising tides of death. But there's a more basic appeal. The play begins powerfully, with the apprehension, the ghost, Hamlet's altercation with Claudius and Gertrude, and Hamlet's encounter with the apparition; the middle part of the action is varied and rapid (the *Mousetrap*, the killing of Polonius, the invective against the queen, the madness of Ophelia); then there's the meditative sequence in the graveyard, culminating in the wild tussle between Laertes and the prince; a brief tranquil phase in which Hamlet accepts almost casually the challenge to the duel; and finally the duel itself, the climactic retribution and the closing obsequies. *Hamlet* is full of contrasting incidents; it's lean, sinewy, mobile, unpadded; even if you think you know it by heart, on stage the action can regain a quality of attack, of surprise, of the unpredictable. There's no character you can trust as a guide; you can't relax into a dominant mood or attitude; one tone is undercut by another, one stance mocked by another; and sententious rhetoric or hyperbolic descriptive set-pieces, which in other Elizabethan plays can become tedious, are here parodied, fragmented, made suspect. There's already, in the stage-play, the vinegary scepticism, the sexual shock-tactics, the abrasive callousness and offhand brutality that our present decadent or disillusioned age finds congenial; but the harshness, ferocity and physicality of much of the action is offset (and therefore accentuated) by the intermingled phases of meditation, introspection and even lyricism. *Hamlet* has a very strong but flexible structure of mutually-reinforcing contrasts; its pacing (now slow, now joltingly rapid), its rhythms (now steady, now flurried and syncopated) and its tones (now quiet, now wildly fervent) work in the theatre as they could never do in the study. Although this is the longest of Shakespeare's plays, its lithe action can make it seem much shorter.

The theatre renders *Hamlet* iconic: a succession of telling and memorable images which impel meanings through the retinas. Sets, costume, gesture and grouping augment the text's visual symbolism. An actor in tinselly finery, playing a king, postures before a false king who is mirrored in the fiction he beholds; Hamlet's satiric feigned madness is challenged by the poignant lunacy of flower-bearing Ophelia; a jester is reduced to a mute skull in the hands of a young prince who once rode on his back; two rivals squabble in a grave, trampling a corpse; a ceremonious duel explodes into mayhem. The audience may have known these scenes already; if the production's any good, it'll make them new: these icons breathe. Literary critics, ancient and modern, often try to assume the authority of moral and political policemen: the text ought to do this, they'll say, or ought not to do that. But the better the play (and the production), the more oblique its relationship to readily-summarisable moral or political positions. It uses them, intersects them, sports with them. The ethical becomes entangled with the aesthetic: what would be horrifying in the street becomes enjoyable on the stage; the play is complexly hypothetical, saying not, 'Confuse me with familiar life', but, 'Enjoy, respond; I evoke, transform and search the familiar; contrast, compare.' The better the production, the more intensive the comparative activity it evokes. Archaic features (ghost, rhyming couplets, rhetorical blank verse, outmoded phrasing) help to construct the ambushes where we are surprised by the fictional revelation of possible real experiences. *Hamlet* can seem linguistically imperialistic, in the sense that it seeks to capture, in words and related gestures, combinations of thought and feeling that previously lurked uncaptured; yet it can seem anti-imperialistic, in the sense that it liberates such combinations of thought and feeling from the empire of inchoate inarticulacy.

Even the best explanatory commentaries on *Hamlet* are inevitably vitiated by their medium of rational expository prose, and though they may explain and extend its meanings for us, they can't reproduce the surprises, ambushes, fusions of old and new, or ferments of rational and emotional. William Shakespeare can sometimes, to modern eyes, appear gross, clumsy, élitist, patriarchal and racially prejudiced; but *Hamlet* retains the power to interrogate *us*; and, in the main, Shakespeare's works offer a supreme example of articulate intelligence, imagination and sensitivity. Measured against that example, the utterances of moralists, politicians and theorists will often seem insufficiently complex and therefore inadequately human. Shakespeare's plays mock the narrowed, partitioned and inflexible selves which ideologists would fabricate. Perhaps his art can still, like Prospero's, waken sleepers from their graves.

CONCLUSION

The risk with explanations of Hamlet which emphasise its lack of co-ordination is that they may underestimate the evidence of high co-ordination; the risk with explanations which emphasise high co-ordination is that they may underestimate the evidence of lack of co-ordination. The borderline between its organisation and disorganisation shifts according to one's mode of scansion. The failing of any single explanation is precisely that it is single and thus neglects other (and sometimes equally or more valid) explanations.

What by now should be obvious is that Hamlet will tantalisingly offer cogent but not conclusive support to many different interpretations. For reasons of economy, vanity or ideology, critics are still rather reluctant to concede that there are many interesting and fruitful options; that the open secret of Hamlet is that it is so constituted as to invite, encourage and reward this diversity; and that its combination of order and muddle, of plenitude and reticence, of eloquent lucidity and silent opacity, denies final confirmation to any single interpretation. This is good, even lifelike, and not something to be feared. Criticism has too long been dominated by the struggle for the right approach, the best theory, the key to the mystery, the solution to the riddle. Critics of Hamlet need, perhaps, to relax into modesty and to turn from the pressure of competition to the pleasure of co-operation. Hamlet is generally rich, full, intelligent; clear in the main, dramatically satisfying; unclear in some features, providing plenty of scope for new interpretations on stage and film as well as in critical essays. It is protean partly by design (clever Shakespeare) and partly by accident (hasty Shakespeare). There is no master-Hamlet to be discovered by poring over the text, and we don't need such a discovery; yet we can hardly shrug our shoulders in resignation, for the pleasure of this play derives largely from our quest to solve its

mysteries, to interrogate its ghost; and if we fail to seek what
it never surrenders, we fail to enjoy what it renders. The
value is that in our pursuit of answers, our search of the play
is simultaneously a searching of life: an exploration of
human identity, character, ethics, psychology, politics,
what you will.

When we look into *Hamlet*, we tend to see ourselves
reflected; and that's because the text has many mirrors built
into it. The prince tells the actors that the purpose of playing
is to 'hold, as 'twere, the mirror up to nature'; and the
mirror of *Hamlet* is multiple, cracked and mobile, so that it
pictures both past and future. If we and our preoccupations
seem reflected in it, that is partly because the play has, to
some degree, made us in its image: Shakespeare's perceptive
eloquence has helped to generate future identities, future
possibilities of living. We all contain more lives within
ourselves than real life permits us to actualise; and
Shakespeare proclaims these covert potentialities by
generating from within himself a Polonius, an Ophelia, a
Claudius, a Gertrude, and, most memorably of all, a Hamlet
whose vitality so copiously exceeds all available roles.

Notes

STAGE HISTORY

1. F. E. Halliday: *Shakespeare and His Critics* (London: Duckworth, 1958), pp. 210–11.
2. F. E. Halliday: *A Shakespeare Companion 1564–1964* (Harmondsworth: Penguin, 1964), p. 204.
3. *Allusions to Shakespeare, A.D. 1592–1693* (London: Trübner, 1886), p. 64.
4. *The Diary of Samuel Pepys*, ed. R. Latham and W. Matthews, Vol. II (London: Bell, 1970), pp. 161, 221; Vol. IV (1971), p. 162; Vol. IX (1976), p. 296; learning 'To be or not to be': Vol. V (1971), p. 321.
5. *Characteristics of Men, Manners, Opinions, Times, etc.* [1711], ed. J. M. Robertson, Vol. I (Gloucester, Mass.: Smith, 1963), p. 180.
6. R. Mander and J. Mitchenson: *Hamlet through the Ages* (London: Rockliff, 1955), p. 24. See also: C. H. Shattuck: 'Shakespeare's Plays in Performance', in *The Riverside Shakespeare* (Boston: Houghton Mifflin, 1974), pp. 1799–1825.
7. *Shakespeare in Perspective*, Vol. I (London: Ariel Books, 1982), p. 191.
8. Roger Manvell: *Shakespeare and the Film* (South Brunswick and New York: Barnes, 1979), p. 134. Peter

Davison's *'Hamlet'*: *Text and Performance* (Houndmills
and London: Macmillan, 1983) describes alternative
interpretations.

CRITICAL HISTORY

1. *Some Remarks on the Tragedy of Hamlet Prince of Denmark*
   . . . . . (London: Wilkins, 1736), pp. 33–4.
2. 'Dissertation sur la tragédie ancienne et moderne', in
   Théâtre de Voltaire (Paris: Garnier, 1874), p. 462.
3. *Johnson on Shakespeare*, ed. Walter Raleigh (London:
   Oxford University Press, 1908), pp. 14, 196.
4. *A Philosophical Analysis and Illustration of Some of
   Shakespeare's Remarkable Characters* (London: Murray,
   1774), Section II, esp. pp. 143, 151–2.
5. 'Criticism on the Character and Tragedy of Hamlet', in
   The Mirror (April 18, 1780), reprinted in *The British
   Essayists*, ed. James Ferguson (London: Richardson *et
   al.*, 1823) p. 260.
6. *Goethes Werke*, Vol. XI (Leipzig: Bibliographisches
   Institut, 1926), p. 247. (My translation.)
7. *Samuel Taylor Coleridge: Shakespearean Criticism*,
   Vol. II, ed. T. M. Raysor (London: Dent, 1960),
   pp. 153, 155.
8. *Hamlet and Don Quixote. An Essay*, tr. Robert Nichols
   (London: Henderson, 1930), p. 11.
9. *La Vie littéraire*, Vol. I (Paris: Calmann-Lévy, 1924),
   pp. 7–8. (My translation.)
10. *Shakespearean Tragedy* [1904] (London: Macmillan,
    1957), pp. 99, 102.
11. *'Hamlet'*: *A Study in Critical Method* (Cambridge:
    Cambridge University Press, 1931), pp. 47, 49.
12. *Ibid.*, p. 66.
13. *Ibid.*, pp. 97–8.
14. L. C. Knights: *Explorations* (Harmondsworth: Penguin,
    1964), p. 16.

15. *Ibid.*, pp. 81, 83, 86–7.
16. G. Wilson Knight: *The Wheel of Fire* (London: Methuen, 1960), pp. 39, 45, 40.
17. Knights, p. 85.
18. T. S. Eliot: *Selected Prose*, ed. John Hayward (Harmondsworth: Penguin, 1953), p. 107. The subsequent quotations are from pp. 107–8.
19. *Ibid.*, p. 139.
20. *Ibid.*, p. 109.
21. *The Complete Psycho-Analytic Works of Sigmund Freud*, Vol. IV (London: Hogarth Press, 1958), p. 265.
22. Ernest Jones: *Hamlet and Oedipus* (London: Gollancz, 1949), pp. 90–91.
23. *Ibid.*, p. 100.
24. *Hamlet's Enemy: Madness and Myth in 'Hamlet'* (London: Vision Press, 1975), p. 113.
25. 'Desire and the Interpretation of Desire in *Hamlet*', in *Literature and Psychoanalysis*, ed. S. Felman (Baltimore and London: Johns Hopkins University Press, 1982), p. 50.
26. '*Hamlet* When New', *Sewanee Review* LXI (1953), p. 21.
27. *Ibid.*, p. 189.
28. *The Messingkauf Dialogues*, tr. John Willett (London: Methuen, 1965), pp. 59–61.
29. *Illusion and Reality* (London: Lawrence & Wishart, 1946), pp. 74–5.
30. *William Shakespeare* (Oxford: Blackwell, 1986), pp. 72, 74.
31. *Shakespeare and the Question of Theory*, ed. P. Parker and G. Hartman (New York and London: Methuen, 1985), pp. 317, 330, 330.
32. Jones, p. 22.

CHAPTER 1

1. *Hamlet*, ed. Harold Jenkins (London and New York:

Methuen, 1982), p. 234 (II.i. 78–81).

2. *William Shakespeare: The Complete Works*, ed. Peter Alexander (London and Glasgow: Collins, 1951), p. 1306.

3. *Narrative and Dramatic Sources of Shakespeare*, ed. Geoffrey Bullough, Vol. VII (London: Routledge & Kegan Paul, 1973), pp. 65–6.

4. *Ibid.*, p. 70.

5. *Ibid.*, p. 110.

6. *Hamlet*, p. 96.

7. *The Complete Works of Thomas Lodge*, Vol. IV (New York: Russell & Russell, 1963), p. 62.

8. References to *The Spanish Tragedy* are to the text in *Five Elizabethan Tragedies*, ed. A. K. McIlwraith (London: Oxford University Press, 1938).

9. Halliday, *Shakespeare and His Critics*, p. 47.

10. *Hamlet*, p. 2.

11. *Hamlet*, p. 34.

12. *Hamlet*, p. 554.

13. See, for example, Roy Battenhouse, 'The Ghost in *Hamlet*: A Catholic "Linchpin"?', *Studies in Philology* XLVIII (1951), pp. 161–92; and Eleanor Prosser, *Hamlet and Revenge* (London: Oxford University Press, 1967).

14. Exodus 20:13; Matthew 5:21 and 5:44; Deuteronomy 32:35; Romans 12:19.

15. Battenhouse, p. 175ff.; *Hamlet*, p. 458.

16. This case will be polemically emphasised towards the end of Chapter 2.

CHAPTER 2

1. The Quarto phrase, 'sleaded pollax', is a notorious crux; some editors read 'sledded Polacks', others 'leaded pole-axe' (I.i. 66).

2. See William Empson, *Seven Types of Ambiguity* (London:

Chatto & Windus, 1953), Chs. 4 and 7.

3. *T. S. Eliot: Selected Prose*, p. 105.
4. See Cedric Watts, *The Deceptive Text* (Brighton: Harvester, 1984), pp. 15 and 35.
5. *Conrad in the Nineteenth Century* (London: Chatto & Windus, 1980), pp. 175–9.
6. Fredson Bowers, *Elizabethan Revenge Tragedy 1587–1642* (Gloucester, Mass.: Smith, 1959), Ch. 1.
7. *Il Principe* (Florence: Sansoni, 1951), p. 149. (My translation.)
8. 'An Essay on Man', I, 290, in *The Poems of Alexander Pope*, ed. John Butt (London: Methuen, 1963), p. 515. Boethius' *De Consolatione Philosophiae* had argued influentially that Fortune's disorder serves God's benign order by deflecting human aspirations from the worldly to the eternal. The less worldly one's goals, the less one is subject to chance.

CHAPTER 3

1. *A Personal Record* [1912] (London: Dent, 1946), p. 35.
2. Ralph Berry, *On Directing Shakespeare* (London: Croom Helm; New York: Barnes and Noble; 1977), p. 13.
3. *Ibid.*, pp. 71–3.
4. *Ibid.*, p. 17.
5. *Ibid.*, p. 38.

Bibliography

(I specify only those texts to which this book is most indebted.)

R. Berry, *On Directing Shakespeare* (London: Croom Helm, 1977).
The Riverside Shakespeare, ed. G. Blakemore Evans (Boston: Houghton Mifflin, 1974).
Fredson Bowers, *Elizabethan Revenge Tragedy 1587–1642* (Gloucester, Mass.: Smith, 1959).
A. C. Bradley, *Shakespearean Tragedy* (London: Macmillan, 1957).
Bertolt Brecht, *The Messingkauf Dialogues* (London: Methuen, 1965).
Narrative and Dramatic Sources of Shakespeare, Vol. VIII, ed. Geoffrey Bullough (London: Routledge & Kegan Paul; New York: Columbia University Press; 1973).
Terry Eagleton, *William Shakespeare* (Oxford: Blackwell, 1986).
T. S. Eliot, *Selected Prose*, ed. John Hayward (Harmondsworth: Penguin, 1953).
William Empson, '*Hamlet* When New', in *Sewanee Review* LXI (1953), pp. 15–42, 185–205.
Terence Hawkes, '*Telmah*', in *Shakespeare and the Question*

of Theory, ed. P. Parker and G. Hartman (New York and London: Methuen, 1985).

Samuel Johnson, *Johnson on Shakespeare*, ed. W. Raleigh (London: Oxford University Press, 1908).

Ernest Jones, *Hamlet and Oedipus* (London: Gollancz, 1949).

Shakespeare: 'Hamlet': A Casebook, ed. John Jump (London: Macmillan, 1968).

G. Wilson Knight, *The Wheel of Fire* (London: Methuen, 1960).

L. C. Knights, *Explorations* (Harmondsworth: Penguin, 1964).

Roger Manvell, *Shakespeare and the Film* (South Brunswick and New York: Barnes, 1979).

William Shakespeare, *Hamlet*, ed. Harold Jenkins (London and New York: Methuen, 1982).

A. J. A. Waldock, *'Hamlet': A Study in Critical Method* (Cambridge: Cambridge University Press, 1931).

Index

(Shakespearian characters are listed individually in this main sequence; themes of Hamlet are listed under 'themes'.)